A TEXT BOOK OF
USER STUDIES AND INFORMETRICS

A TEXT BOOK OF USER STUDIES AND INFORMETRICS

P. BALASUBRAMANIAN
M.A., M.B.A., M.C.A., M.L.I.Sc., M.Phil., Ph.D.
University Librarian & Head
Department of Library and Information Science
Manonmaniam Sundaranar University
Tirunelveli-62712, Tamil Nadu, India

P. VIJI
M.B.A, M.L.I.Sc,(NET), PhD
Librarian, Ambai Arts College
Ambasamudram,Tirunelveli- 627401

E. SANTHANA KUMAR
B.Sc, M.Lib.I.Sc, PhD, Research Scholar
Department of Library and Information Science
Manonmaniam Sundaranar University
Tirunelveli-62712

Ess Ess Publications
New Delhi

A TEXT BOOK OF
USER STUDIES AND INFORMETRICS

Copyright © by Authors

All rights reserved. No part of this book may be reproduced in any form or by any electronic or mechanical means including information storage and retrieval systems without permission in writing from the publisher, except by a reviewer, who may quote brief passages in a review.

While extensive effort has gone into ensuring the reliability of information appearing in this book, the publisher makes no warranty, express or implied on the accuracy or reliability of the information, and does not assume and hereby disclaims any liability to any person for any loss or damage caused by errors or omissions in this publication.

ISBN : 978-81-947398-0-7

Price : Rs. 1000/-

First Published 2021

Published by:
Ess Ess Publications
4831/24, Ansari Road,
Darya Ganj,
New Delhi-110 002.
INDIA
Phones: 23260807, 41563444
Fax: 41563334
E-mail: info@essessreference.com
www.essessreference.com

Cover Design by *Patch Creative Unit*

Printed and bound in India

Contents

Preface
Acknowledgements

Unit 1   **1-40**

    Ascertain the user of a library/information system/service;
    Understand the purposes/goals of user studies
    Importance of user studies
    Need for conducting user studies
    Major user studies conducted in India

Unit 2   **41-96**

    Sprouting theory of user behaviour
    Analysing the factors influencing the user behaviour
    Limitations in behavioural research
    Aim and objectives of User needs and user education
    Planning of user education
    Problems of user studies and user education.

Unit 3   **97-136**

    Growth and development of the concept of informetrics
    Understand the term librametrics, Biometrics and Scientometrics
    Evolution of Classic Informetric Laws
    Implications of Informetric Laws
    Understood New trends in Informetrics

Unit 4   **137-204**

    To understand the Quantitative and Qualitative techniques

To classify the Cluster analysis, Correspondence analysis & Coward analysis

To study the impact of media and audience analysis

To know about SPSS.11.0 version

Unit 5 205-268

To understand the Citation Analysis

To know the different forms of citations

Citation counts & Self –citation

Application of Quantitative and Qualitative techniques in LIS Research

To explore parametric and non-parametric tools.

Preface

The main purpose of writing this book is to understand more about User Studies and Informetrics. In this book, we have incorporated various concepts regarding methods of user studies and recent trends in the user studies in India as well as the international scenario. We have also attempted to highlight user behaviour with support of various user behaviour theories.

We have put in our sincere effort and time to make this book very useful to readers and simple to understand. We hope the readers find it worth reading. All the constructive feedback is cordially invited.

Suggestions for improvement of this book would be highly appreciated.

P. Balasubramanian
P. Viji
E. Santhana Kumar

Acknowledgements

The authors feel extremely indebted to Dr K. Pitchumani, Hon'ble Vice-Chancellor, Manonmaniam Sundaranar University, Tirunelveli. We also thank Dr.A. Palavesam, Registrar, Manonmaniam Sundaranar University, Tirunelveli and all teaching and non-teaching staff members of the Manonmaniam Sundaranar University, for giving us constant encouragement in writing this book.

We acknowledge our heartfelt gratitude to Dr R. Sevukan Associate Professor Department of Library & Information Science Pondicherry University, Pondicherry and Dr M.Veliah, Self-Finance Director, Ambai Arts College, Ambasamudram.

We acknowledge the services of Ess Ess Publications, New Delhi for their efforts in bringing out this book in a record time. Suggestions for improvement of the book are most welcome.

P. Balasubramanian
P.Viji
E. Santhana Kumar

Unit 1

OBJECTIVES
- Ascertain the user of a library/information system/service;
- Understand the purposes/goals of user studies
- Importance of user studies
- Need for conducting user studies
- Major user studies conducted in India

1.1. INTRODUCTION

Users constitute an inseparable and indispensable part of any library and information system. The emergence of an information organisation is due to the very essence of the users. Users for a library are the all-important factors and the most vital component without which a library loses the whole purpose because it is for them only, the libraries are existing, and established and maintained. In the context of library and information centres, it is extremely important to understand who the users are, what their needs are, and how these needs can effectively be met, addressed, and be satisfied by the library. It is presumed that, if a library is not being used by users enough, it is probably because users are not being taken care of enough by the library. Hence, proper emphasis should be given on users through the conduct of user studies, periodical assessment of their information needs at given intervals.

There are various terms such as user, client, and patron which are being often used interchangeably by the LIS researchers with the term user. H. Julien (1999) has categorized these synonym terms as follows:

(a) User

This is the term that is generally employed to refer to clients of information services and libraries, and participants or respondents' in research studies.

(b) Client

This term suggests a particular type of professional relationship often used by the people in the Judiciary.

(c) Customer

This term is associated with a business model of service provisions that invokes notions of financial transactions and often insists on the introduction of corporate culture in library services.

(d) Patron

This term elicits images of wealthy benefactors and guardians which implies a kind of respect and esteem for the library members.

But it is quite difficult to exactly define the library user by applying any one of the single terms since they cannot fully explain who the users of a library are. Michael Gorman (1983) while attempting to define the term, "users" coined a term, "Library". which was considered by many as "hideous" and was rejected. However, different authors who put their efforts to define the phrase, "library users" differently as an alternative term for users, but no consensus opinion seem to have been evoked in the field for uniform use.

Although there are no generally accepted definitions on the user, the term has become one of the most prominent terminologies on which the very existence of the whole library system depends. It is a fact that the whole spectrum of the library system and services are directed towards users. The whole effort, energy, and money involved in building up the library become futile unless a library system assesses the actual information requirements of its potential users. Thus, to create a good library and information environment and to make the library services more effective and meaningful, library researchers have concentrated their research more on user studies than any other field of librarianship.

1.2. USER STUDIES: CONCEPT AND MEANING

The role of the library as a social and service institution catering to the information need of its users is being recognized widely the world over. The library professionals are primarily concerned with the needs of the users for whom the library exists. Therefore, user studies are considered as an important stigma of library usage.

Several libraries and information scientists/researchers have defined the phrase "user study" in their ways realizing, the importance of the concept in the contemporary library World. Girija Kumar (1989) defines the phrase, "User Study" as the diagnostic studies for discovering the causal relationship between the user of information and the information system. According to Lahiri (1990), 'user studies are often instigated as attempts to understand, justify, explain, or expand the real library usage and, consequently to gain more knowledge about the process of communication concerning their libraries and their respective clientele. However, Sangameswaram and Gopinath (1987) have defined the concept differently as the user studies are hardly restricted to the actual or potential user alone as several studies have also been made on non-users who constitute a major chunk of the users 'population of a given library.

User studies were originated with the perception that one could design an effective information system by understanding user's needs and information use. Nowadays, user studies are more refined by using more sophisticated techniques (both sociological and technological) and focusing more on system-oriented studies.

User studies, use studies, information need studies, communication behaviour studies, information dissemination, and utilization studies, user-research, etc. are conceptually synonymous and as such are complementary to each other and closely related often, but not precisely defined. The reason is that the terminology depends much on the approach and the angle from which it is seen. There are several overlapping facets included in these studies. As such, the scope of user-studies is enormous and user components will have bearing on almost all aspects of the library and information system. The ultimate aim of user studies is to help in designing, altering, evaluating, and improving the efficiency and effectiveness of library and information systems and their services.

It is also important to look into the various limitations of use and user studies. User studies may not reveal the spillover effects of use, indirect use of a library, and several fruitful interactions of users with the library. Further, the use of the library and its utility to users are often quite different. A library may be used but it may not be useful, another may be useful but may not be used, the third one may neither useful nor used and, the ideal is one which is both used and useful remarks Sridhar (2002).

1.3. S.R. RANGANATHAN'S FIVE LAWS OF LIBRARY SCIENCE AND USER STUDIES

The concept of 'User Study' prevail in the five laws of Library Science of S.R. Ranganathan. Let us see how they depict it by asking questions while assessing the users;

- Books are for use - Are library's certain services available for use
- Every user his/her book- Whether the information desired by you is available in the library
- Every book its user- Whether the existing services used by you
- Save the time of user- Whether the services/information reaches on time
- A library is a growing organism - Whether the collection/services is/are adequate

Hence the history of user studies has roots in Ranganathan's five laws of library science, 1931.

1.4. NEED FOR THE USER STUDIES

In the field of medical practice, large-scale clinical trials, and systematic reviews of those clinical trials are regularly conducted in support of "evidence-based medicine" [Cochrane Collaboration, 2003; Cochrane, 1972]. This concept has already been applied to the practice of medical librarianship [Eldredge, 2000] and other areas of librarianship

[Dahlgreen, 2002; Marshall, 2003; Williams, 2002]. By using empirical evidence as to the basis for decision making in library management, we have the potential to make great strides forward in the practice of librarianship. In other words, if we know more about the people that our libraries and information centres serve, it is much more likely that we can serve them effectively.

The reasons for conducting user studies are varied and many. The question regarding the need for user study remains mostly undebated among the L&IS researchers. The user study would be valueless if sufficient reasons are not provided for conducting user studies satisfactorily. For any library and information system, 'use' is the main purpose and "user" is the most valuable and key component. User-oriented approach, design, and evaluation are the basic necessity for libraries to make their systems and services more effective and user-friendly. Hence, user studies are a must at the time of designing a library system or initiation of new library services. The effectiveness of the library and information system depends on the extent to which the system characteristics correspond with the users, and in how much the potential users are willing and able to make use of it. The library authorities, administrators, planners, and managers of library and information systems have to consider the role of users in the utilization of information properly. User studies can also stem from the efforts of the evaluation of a system or service.

In the opinion of Sangameswar and Gopinath (1987), five vital reasons make user studies exigent. These include

- To identify the potential users and to categorize them;
- To identify their information requirements by the class of information needed and the level and type of communication media required;
- To identify the existing resources and services to achieve the comprehensiveness of information even without unwanted duplication of efforts

- To evaluate various existing services about their utility to their users to effect suitable modifications and to introduce new services as and when necessary, and finally,
- To achieve overall improvements in the parent library system from the feedback obtained".

A systematic user study can also, reveal some anticipated data about the dynamic component of a user. It may also help to start a new service for users, which may be extremely useful for them. Further, as no library and information system has unlimited financial provisions, users' studies are required to check whether intended goals are served by them or not. If required, the priorities and programmes can be altered to ensure the judicious allocation of the limited library fund. User studies are also required not only to determine and confirm the general patterns of use of libraries but also to identify the lacunae inherent in the existing library system and services.

1.5. OBJECTIVES OF USER STUDIES:

Some of the important reasons/ objectives for which libraries and information centres/researchers conduct users' studies can be summarized as follows.

- To identify the potential users and their information need;
- To identify the information-seeking behaviour of users;
- To ascertain about the perception and approaches of users towards information;
- To identify the weakness and strength of existing library resources and services;
- To evaluate the library system i.e. how far the existing library system and services can meet the information needs of its 'users

- To specify the problems and limitations of the library which may discourage the users to use the library;
- To identify the attitude of library staff towards users in providing information;
- To understand the level of participation of users in building a good library environment;
- To analyze the initiation of some new library services for users;
- To improve the overall system and services of the library;
- To build up user-friendly resource collection.

The above reasons are quite pragmatic to make the library environment more clientele-friendly and purposive. The basic necessity of such studies is to make a detailed study on users, their information needs, their approaches towards information need, and match their requirements with existing library systems and services to develop the overall library system. Another benefit of user studies is that a new library system and services can be implemented in the library or introduced and collection policy can be modified, keeping in view the users existing and future requirements. User studies help to improve the public relations of a library with its users. To summarize, it can be stated that users' studies are a means of continuous 'librarian education' about users and their information needs.

1.6. USER STUDIES AND SURVEYS

In the early years' user studies "research was conducted which later shifted from studies of library and documentation used to user behaviour or the information behaviour, information-seeking behaviour. The term user study means a study of user's need for information. The purpose of user study is to attempt to discover patterns of use and levels of awareness of users towards library services and facilities, to determine success or non-success of services and to identify what adjustments are needed in service strategy. According to Busha and Harter (1980) "User studies are often instigated as attempts to understand justify explain or expand library usage and consequently to gain more knowledge about the process of communication in so far as libraries and their clientele are concerned". According to Kamaruddin (1992), a user study is a systematic study of the information requirements of users in facilitating exchanges between information system and users. Pao (1989) grouped user studies in three stages:

1. User-oriented studies
2. System use oriented studies
3. Utility oriented studies

User-oriented studies focused on characteristics of users and Pao (1989) considers points in this study are age, educational level, task description etc. System use oriented studies drive their data from the system. The transactions between users and the system are investigated and examined like a loan through ILL, the number of online searches performed. Utility oriented studies are reflected in information use and this impact. The purpose of user study is:

- To identify the needs of users
- To identify the resources and services needs of users
- To identify the strength and weakness of library resources
- For collection development
- For proper resources collection.
- A user study is a complex process as it holds studies of information needs, information use,

ISB, use of information sources and channels. Accessing information needs and ISB is the base for designing information systems and services. Information provider cannot provide information unless he knows or identifies the need and expectation of users. The "Centre for Research on

User Studies" defines user study as a "multidisciplinary art of knowledge being the study of the behaviour of users (and non-users) of information systems and services." User studies are concerned with analysing people, their attitude, priorities, preferences and behaviour. The main steps involved in user studies are selection and formulation of the research problem, working hypothesis, literature search, overall design or planning the strategy of the study, sampling and sampling strategy or plan, data collection, measurement and scaling techniques, interpretation, generalization and realization of objectives, preparation, writing, presentation and dissemination of research results etc. Thus, user studies are considered as attempts to understand justify, explain or expand library information sources and services usage.

Information sources are more complex and expensive and beyond reach to stack at one place. The traditional collection is in print form and services based on it are reference service, current awareness services and selective dissemination of information. These services are to be supplemented by just for your services instead of just in case or just in time. The increased use of technology and availability of e-resources in all sectors including LIC is experienced and has forced both users and librarians to shift the practices. The basic challenge for library professionals is to convince and convert traditional users into users of internet-based resources, e-resources and services based on these media. Thirunavukkarasu (2011) indicated the future of libraries and pointed out that college and university libraries face enormous challenges and opportunities to manage user demands and expectations. As campuses move into the information age, mission and role of the library are being redefined. The number of information libraries needs to acquire continues to increase but it is not sufficient to fulfil user needs despite heavy investment in the collection development. The users require information from the library, which is current, accurate, relevant, comprehensive and useful. This can be successfully possible by incorporating end-users survey or analysis of needs and users, in any type of libraries. The term user study has been defined variously by different information scientists. According to Vikas user studies or use studies could be concerned with the study of information processing activities of the users. Empirical studies on the use of demand or need for information is usually called user studies. A study, which is focused on users to understand directly or indirectly their information needs, use behaviours and use patterns, is termed as user study. The term user studies are referred to library surveys because of studies of information needs or information use behaviour focus upon a wider range of information sources and channels rather than simply libraries. User studies comprise the study of people's need for and use of information. A user study may be defined as the systematic study of information requirements of users to facilitating meaningful exchange between information systems and users. User studies cover aspects like user behaviour, the use of literature and information sources consulted, etc.

The reasons for conducting user studies are:

1. To identify the actual strengths and weaknesses of library resources and services
2. To identify the levels and kinds of user needs
3. To identify faculty and student priorities for use of library resources and services
4. To identify the limitations or problems in the use of information resources
5. To improve the organization and planning of library services.
6. To find out the information-seeking attitudes of users
7. To find out users' requirement and expectations from the library, in terms of type, quality and range of services to satisfy their needs.

The different types of user studies put forth by Wilson-Davis are as follows: Library oriented studies: investigates the use of individual library or information centres. User-oriented studies: studies based on how a particular user group obtains information needed to conduct any work. Categories of user studies discussed by Menzel are also summarized below:

User studies try to find out the relative use of different channels of information in response to various questions.

Behaviour studies: these studies are carried out to find the pattern of overall reaction of the user community to the communication system without any reference to any specific information receiving the event. In such studies, the communication behaviour of users is studied.

Information flow studies: This types of study views the pattern of flow of information in the communication system (From manuscript to print and publication).

Channel studies: involve a thorough study of a particular information channel used by scientists or users. The channels may be primary or secondary or tertiary resources.

Critical incident technique: this type of study takes a particular incident in the information-seeking activities of a scientist and studies that incident critically. It tries to find out how and when the incident occurred, what information need arose, what steps were taken to meet the need, whether the user was satisfied with the information obtained and whether the results of information collected may affect his work.

Dissemination studies: It studies the type of information produced by the users, how the information reaches them and its utility. These views regarding use studies indicate that the purpose is to identify the use pattern of users while searching for information. These studies analyse the use pattern of information sources by the users.

1.7. METHODS OF USER STUDIES

It is not enough to design and carry out a user study just as a vague desire to know more about the users whom the library serves and their information needs. For each user study, there is a need to formulate a specific question that will be answered by the results of that study. Reviewing existing studies on related issues provides some valuable guidance in this regard.

Among various methods advocated, the survey method is the most popular and extensively accepted in user studies. In this method, the sample of individuals having worked in a specific field or experience is requested to provide certain information. The response obtained from them are critically analyzed and examined in light of the proposed hypotheses. The following criteria can be taken into consideration at the time of surveying users.

It is necessary to determine the three basic objectives of the library and information system to evaluate the decision making process and assessing the effectiveness of a given library system. Also, the level of success of various programmes and services are evaluated to modify the existing programmes and designing new programmes and services, thereby to overcome the existing deficiencies of the library and information system;

It is imperative to determine the level of users' satisfaction and attitudes. Also, it is necessary to identify the potential and actual users along with their information needs and preferences. All these will help to establish user interaction with the system more effectively; and

In the survey method, although user characteristics play an important role, other factors like users' interest, lifestyle, literature use habit, etc. are more crucial for taking an appropriate decision and/or to engineer the system.

Libraries use various methods to carry out user studies.

These methods are direct and indirect. Direct methods are based on establishing contact with the users and active involvement of the users under study. While, indirect methods are based on the library's analysis of its records and other sources, without the involvement of the users under study.

1.7a Indirect Methods

Many libraries depend on analysis of their records and statistics, like, circulation records, reservation records, reference query files, etc. to assess the information requirements of their users. These methods are known as indirect methods. Library records provide useful information. For example, records of reference questions and literature search can give an insight into the type of queries received, type of documents used and time taken to answer a question, etc. Similarly, circulation record can be analyzed to determine the activity of the library as well as to determine the reading habits of library users. Indirect methods provide useful information. However, for finding views of the user, indirect methods are not appropriate. For example, indirect methods cannot provide information related to the user's views about library services and his/her attitude, opinion, or preferences or behaviour as an individual. It thus becomes necessary to observe or question them directly

Direct methods of user studies involve the participation of the users under study. Most of the general methods and techniques of social surveys, such as questionnaire, interview, diaries, observations, etc. are direct methods. You will learn these methods in the following sections

1.7.1a. Questionnaire Method

Several other methods are followed in user studies such as questionnaire method, personal interview, observation, telephonic survey, analysis of library records, citation analysis, etc. Among all these methods, the questionnaire method is normally regarded as an important and impersonal survey method. In this method, a predefined set of questions are asked to a specifically defined group of users either through mail or personally, and the users are asked to answer the questions. The questionnaire method seems to be the most commonly accepted device to conduct user studies and is also considered as the most suitable and convenient method due to its lower cost, greater autonomy, and accessibility particularly when the users are geographically dispersed. By applying this technique, the researcher Can collect detailed information about users' habits, perceptions on the functioning of the library, and opinion on impressing the standard of existing library services. The vital limitation of this method is the rate of response which is one of the key constraints for any researcher not only in the field of library and information science but also in the entire spectrum of social research. There are three basic types of questionnaires, closed-ended open-ended, and a combination of both.

1.7.1b. Closed-ended questionnaire

Closed-ended questionnaires generally include multiple-choice questions or scale questions. This type of questionnaire can be, administered to a large number of respondents or sample sizes. As there is a set format, the data generated from the questionnaire can be easily fed into a computer system for analysis.

1.7.1c. Open-ended questionnaire

Open-ended questionnaires offer the flexibility to respondents to answer in their own words. It may leave a blank section to write an answer. Closed-end questionnaires might be used to find out how many people use metro rail service in New Delhi, but open-ended questionnaires might be used to find out what people think about the quality of service.

1.7.1d. Combined questionnaire

In this method, it is possible to find out how many people

use the service and what they think of the service in the same form. The combined questionnaire may begin with a series of closed-end questions, with boxes to tick or scales to rank, and then finish with a section of open-ended questions or more detailed response.

Advantages of Questionnaire method: It is experienced that the majority of the investigators follow the questionnaire method as an important technique of data collection. Some of the reasons may be as follows:

- It is a simple and convenient method of data collection.
- When the population is large and dispersed geographically, this method is useful.
- It is economical and fast.

Disadvantages : This method has the following disadvantages also:

- The response level is usually low.
- Due to poorly phrased questions, respondents may not be able to answer them.
- Difficult to verify the information provided by the respondents.

1.7.2. Personal Interview Method

A personal interview, which is one of the convenient ways to make user study is a face to face interpersonal role situation. In this method, the interviewer asks questions to the respondents to obtain answers pertinent to the formulated hypotheses. The most important thing in this method is that, how relevant and accurate the questions are structured. Among structured and unstructured interviews, the structured interview involves the use of a set of a predetermined set of questions and a highly standardized technique of recording, whereas the unstructured interview appears to be the central technique of collecting information on research studies. In the interview, most of the time the users reveal data on both user and non-user attitudes and their behaviour. Also, the answer often provides the greatest amount of probing and answer-seeking.

Advantages : Personal Interview Method has the following advantages:
- It is simple and easy to perform.
- It is quick to be used.
- The response rate is usually high.
- Can cover a wide geographical area.
- Possible to obtain a complete response.

Disadvantages : This method also has the following disadvantages:
- It is time-consuming and uneconomical.
- Conducting an interview requires some training.
- Respondents have little time to think.
- Sometimes responses may be difficult to analyze.

1.7.3. Diary Method

This is another conventional method of data collection that is used in survey research. In this method, the respondents under study are asked to keep a detailed record of particular events, information activities, such as information research, reading, browsing, literature search, and so on. These are problems that involve human behaviour, i.e. the users keep a record of their activities and behaviour. The record is maintained in the diaries given to the respondents over some time, rather than on a single occasion. This method is used for items that are easily forgotten, whether because they are insignificant (for a particular study), or because they occur frequently. After the study is complete, the diaries are returned to the investigator for analysis.

Advantages : The advantages of this method are as follows:

- It is useful for recording events that may be difficult to recall at a later time.
- It is useful to find out an aspect of users' behaviour that may change over time.
- It can be used in situations where observation may not be practical.

Disadvantages : Diary Method has the following disadvantages also:
- Difficult to obtain a running record from the busy respondents.
- When a user's library use is being investigated, he may change his usual patterns.
- Difficult to persuade users to keep a diary, hence a representative sample may not be available.

1.7.4. Observation Method : For user study, another important method is the observation method which is considered the most basic, primitive, and widely accepted modern method. Even though it is mostly used in scientific research, in the library environment, user study can be undertaken in observing phenomena primarily associated with the library use information concerning different behavioural patterns of library users which can be collected in the library by observation without involving the users directly. The most common types of user studies conducted in the library by observation methods include the use of card catalogue, types of reference queries, circulation of library materials, type of questions being asked to the reference desk, and their approach to various information sources, etc.

Characteristics of the observation method : Observation as a method of data collection has certain characteristics.
- It is both a physical and mental activity. The observing eye 'catches' many things which are slighted, but the

attraction is focused on data that are pertinent to the given study.

- Observation is selective. The researcher does not observe anything and everything but selects the range of things to be observed based on the nature, scope, and objectives of his study
- Observation is purposive and not casual. It is made for the specific purpose of nothing things relevant to the study.
- It captures the natural social context in which persons' behaviour occurs.
- It grasps the significant events and occurrences that affect the social relations of the participants.
- Observation should be exact and be based on standardized tools of research such as observation schedule, social-metric scale, and precision instruments if any.

1.7.5. Types of observation

Observation may be classified in different ways. About the investigator's role, it may be classified into (a) participant observation, and (b) non-participant observation, in terms of mode of observation, it may be classified into (c) direct observation and (d) indirect observation. Concerning the rigour of the system adopted, observation is classified into (e) controlled observation, and (f) uncontrolled observation.

(a) Participant observation : In this observation, the observer is a part of the phenomena or group which is observed and he acts as both an observer and a participant. The persons who are observed should not be aware of the researcher's purpose. Then only their behaviour will be 'natural'. The concealment of the research objective and researcher's identity is justified on the ground that it makes it possible to study certain aspects of the group's culture which are not revealed to outsiders makes it possible to study certain aspects of the group's culture which are not revealed to outsiders.

(b) Non-participant observation : In this method, the observer stands apart and does not participate in the phenomenon observed. Naturally, there is no emotional involvement on the part of the observer. This method calls for skill in recording observations in an unnoticed manner.

(c) Direct observation : This means observation of an event personally by the observer when it takes place. This method is flexible and allows the observer to see and record subtle aspects of events and behaviour as they occur. He can free to shift places, change the focused of the observation. A limitation of this method is that the observer's perception circuit may not be able to cover all relevant events when the latter move quickly, resulting in the incompleteness of the observation.

(d) Indirect observation : This does not involve the physical presence of the observer, and the recording is done by mechanical, photographic, or electronic devices. This method is less flexible than direct observation, but it is less biasing and less erratic in recording accuracy. It also provides a permanent record for an analysis of different aspects of the event.

(e) Controlled observation : This involves the standardization of observational technique and exercise of maximum control over extrinsic and intrinsic variables by adopting experimental design and systematically recording observations. Controlled observation is earned out either in the laboratory or in the field. It is typified by clear and explicit decisions on what, how, and when to observe. It is primarily used for inferring causality, and testing the causal hypothesis.

(f) Uncontrolled observation : This does not involve control over extrinsic and intrinsic variables. It is primarily used for descriptive research. Participant observation is a typical uncontrolled one.

Advantages: The advantages of this method include the following:
- Useful to study the actual behaviour of the respondents.
- The data collected is more reliable.
- It is not biased.

Disadvantages : The disadvantages include the following:
- It is a time-consuming method.
- The duration of activity may either be very long or too short to observe properly.
- Sometimes difficult to quantify human behaviour

1.7.6. Telephonic Survey Method

A telephonic Survey is another method of a survey of users, conducted through a telephonic interview. This method is considered as a semi-personal method of collecting information that has gained general acceptance as a substitute for a personal interview. The telephonic survey method is gaining wide popularity as it is convenient to conduct, cost-effective, and has a higher rate of response.

In the opinion of Nachmias and Nachmias (1991), although there are several methods followed for User studies, three major methods seem to be popularly used to elicit information from respondents such as Personal Interview, the Questionnaire, and the Telephone Survey.

However, Guha (1983) has grouped all the existing techniques employed in user studies into three broad categories as follows:
- General or Conventional Method;
- Indirect Method; and

1.7.6a. General or Conventional Method

This category includes methods like- questionnaires, interviews, diary, the observation by self, etc. Among these methods, questionnaire and interview methods are found to be more popular compared to other methods due to their cost-effectiveness and geographical constraints.

1.8. INDIRECT METHOD

As the name implies, this method helps to collect data on user studies indirectly without making direct contact with the users. It includes methods primarily citation analysis and analysis of library records.

1.8.1. Citation analysis or bibliometric study

This is an indirect, but popular, method of user studies. It analyses the bibliographic citations appended to their documents (journal articles, theses, books, etc.) by authors. It provides useful data on the types of documents used and cited by the authors. The citations or references provided by authors become the basis of citation analysis. It explains that the documents cited by the authors are used by them; hence it is an indication as to the nature of materials required by library users. Citation analysis proves helpful to the librarian to decide on the acquisition of documents, selection or rejection of material used for developing an information service or product, etc. This method is also found to be useful in determining the non-use of a significant proportion of journals; hence library can review its journal subscription policy.

Advantages : Citation analysis has the following advantages:
- It is regarded as an unbiased method.
- It helps to produce a rank list of journals thus helping in their acquisition.
- It also provides useful indicators for identifying institutions of excellence, individual experts, etc.

In the opinion of Devarajan (1989) "though citation analysis is mostly viewed as unbiased in comparison to other methods, it gives rise to several perils. These are as follows:

- It gives only a partial idea about the use of secondary and tertiary sources, formal and informal sources, etc. which are not cited by the authors;
- Citation studies are not always good indicators of the actual use of journals.
- There is a possibility of citing unused documents of reputed authors.
- The possibility of self-citation by certain authors

1.8.2. Analysis of Library Records

This method ascertains the users' information requirements indirectly. It involves the analysis of statistical records maintained in a library which can provide a view of the information needs of the user community. It includes the analysis of important library records such as circulation records, interlibrary loan records, reference query request records, and so on. Analysis of these records reveals the nature of the use of the documents, types of reference questions asked effectiveness of reference and information services, etc.

Advantages

- It is useful in determining the policies of the library regarding collections, services, etc.
- It is useful in the computerization of library in-house activities.
- It can help to enhance the efficiency and effectiveness of library services

1.9. SPECIAL AND UNCONVENTIONAL METHODS

The unconventional method includes computer feedback which makes use of records generated from the result of a computer search. This technique is gaining popularity by libraries due to the emergence and introduction of modem technologies in libraries for various purposes. This method helps the researchers to know about the various formal and informal channels of communication to make their studies effective and meaningful.

Paisley (1968) described it as "the methodology for gathering information about information use pattern in a different fashion". They have grouped the unconventional method into three broad categories such as:

- by asking people about it;
- by observing its occurrence; and
- by examining its artefacts.

Similarly, Maheswarappa and Hiremath (1995) have opined that unconventional methods can be used either individually or in a combination of two or more methods depending upon the nature and scope of the problem and the number of users to be studied.

The study of different methods stated above clearly reveals that every method has its advantages and limitations. Hence, the researchers engaged in user studies should be extremely careful in choosing a method suitable for his/her studies taking the nature and composition of users and the environment into account.

1.10. MAJOR USER STUDIES IN INDIA

User Study' is a difficult area of knowledge to define. It can include a traditional or conventional survey of library borrowers and it may be the main form of activity that comes to mind when the term 'user studies' is mentioned. A study entitled "Pilot Study on the use of scientific literature by scientists" conducted by Ralph R. Shaw (1956) is considered a pioneer study in this direction. There was comprehensive bibliography on user studies compiled by Davis and Bailin 1964 containing 438 studies. One of the turning points in the history of user studies was the establishment of the "Centre for Research on User Studies" (CRUS) in 1975 at the University of Sheffield. The purpose of the centre is to create a national centre to act as a focus for research in user studies. User studies have many impacts on library services and systems. User studies are directly or indirectly, playing a pivotal role in systems and services, such as collection development, resource allocation, improvement of library techniques, etc.

A significant effort was made by INSDOC (now NISCAIR) and conducted a Use Survey entitled "INSDOC List of Current Scientific Literature" in 1964. After that INSDOC compiled "Indian Science Abstracts". IASLIC conducted a seminar on "User and Library and Information Services", and pay attention to users. In the year 1967, INSDOC conducted a pilot survey to access the information needs of the researchers of electronics. One pioneer study was conducted by M. S. Sridhar. This study was conducted on ISRO Satellite Centre (ISAC), Bangalore. The results of this doctoral work have been published under the title "Information Behaviour of Scientists and Engineers". The user studies take an exponential growth in recent years. It can be easily found in the literature of library and information science that majority of researches leading to M. Phil. and Ph. D. Degree are conducted on user studies.

1.10.1. Academic Libraries

Numerous studies in the field of academic libraries were conducted in recent years.

Carl M. White's study at the University of Delhi Library in 1965 was the first of its kind in India which gave a detailed account of the library development in regards to its services. No definite standard for use in developing a university library program exists. Among other things, the quality aspects of the library development rather than the 'users approach' seem to have been predetermined in his recommendations.

Krishna Kumar's study (1973) on the use of Sapru House Library serving Social Science teachers and scholars provides sufficient clue concerning the average number of days and hours the library is put to use, along with the priority of information sources being explored, thereby giving scope for the library administrator to reorient the library system suitable to the requirements of Social Scientists. Dhani conducted a survey of 100 readers at Rajasthan University Library in 1974 which revealed that readers demonstrated their interest more in using the library at the college level with an optimal approach to the library catalogue and handling reference books. The study stressed the need for user education for the new entrants of the college library.

"Information Seeking behaviour of the academics of the University of Kerala in the changed Library Environment" by Shibu Rays and M. D. Baby (2011) reveals that academics have welcomed the automation of library, and a shift towards electronic information seeking is visible, which implies that ICT has an impact on the information-seeking behaviour of the academics. "Information seeking behaviour of the academics in Government Colleges in changing scenario" by Jogender Singh (2010) concludes that academics have welcomed the automation of the library. Some remarkable studies in this field are "Use of library resources in university libraries by the students" by Md. Sohail and others (2012), "User perception and use of library and information services in the higher research and academic institutions in Lucknow city" by K. L. Mahawar (2011), "Uses of e-journals by researchers in AMU" by M. M. Raza and A. K. Upadhyay (2006), etc.

The well-known user studies in this field were conducted by P. Geeth (2003), Varghese (2006), M. S. Lohar and T. N. Roopashree (2006), Lalitha K. Sami and Rabia Iffat (2009), D B. Patil and S. Parameshwar (2009), Y. Srinivasa Rao and B. K. Choudhury (2008), B. U. Kannapanavar and K. V. Manjunatha (2010), B. D. Kambar and Gururaj Hadagali (2009) entitled "Use of UGC-INFONET journal consortium by faculty members and research scholars of Karnataka University" etc.

1.10.2. Special Libraries

Many studies have been conducted in the past to assess the information requirements of scientists, engineers, and technologists. The important findings of some of the studies are below:

"Use of electronic resources by research scholars in CFTRI, Mysore: A study (2005) by Mallinath Kumbar and others. It is clear from the study that how electronic resources are useful to research scholars. This study helps the librarians in planning and developing electronic resources in providing modern services to their library users. Another important study entitled "Information used pattern of social scientists: An analysis of citation of journals of Asian studies" (2007) by Neena Talwar Kanungo. The study highlights the low use of electronic sources can be a good area of research in the future. The accessibility of online electronic sources should be more utilized by social scientists. good area of research in the future. The accessibility of online electronic sources should be more utilized by social scientists.

Some remarkable studies in a various allied field such as forestry were carried out by T. Hazarika (2005) entitled "Information use pattern of Indian forestry scientists: A bibliometric study". M. Ahmad and S. Haridasam (2006) carried out the user survey on "Use of the periodical by scholars at National Library of Veterinary Science". Another study on this subject was carried out by Biswas and Enamul Haque (2008). In recent years' user study on special Organisations was also noticed. Mahawar and others (2009) studied "Information seeking behaviour of Geologist". "Information seeking behaviour of users of the cyber library: A case study of Tata Institute of Social Science" by Kiran Kaushik and others (2011). The study revealed that the cyber library was extensively used by male users as compared to the female users and users preferred using a particular database only.

1.10.3. Digital Libraries

Today in the library and information centres various kinds of electronic resources have been produced by applying modern IT. The commonly available electronic sources are competing with and in some instances replacing, the print-based information sources, which have been in place as the primary media for storage and communication of recorded information. Because of this reason, many user studies in this field were conducted by Lohar and Roopashree (2006), D. B. Patil (2009), A. Manimekali (2006), S. Patil (2007), Y. Srinivasa Rao (2008), Rama Devi (2006), Lalitha K. Sami (2009), etc. One remarkable study was carried out by Sadanand Y. Bansode and Shamin Periera (2008), entitled "A survey of library automation in college libraries in Goa State" concluded that the library automation began in 1970 in a few special libraries and has now reached most of University library. It due to various problems many college libraries in India have yet to take off India.

1.11. RECENT USER STUDIES

International Scenario

The upcoming trend in user studies as a result of technological advances and changes in the economics of information systems. Modern digital libraries have multiple diverging requirements and expectations of the users and rapidly changing technological innovations. Many studies have looked into digital libraries in a specific context. Bishop (1999), Covi and Kling (1997) studied the use of digital libraries by people from different social and economic backgrounds. Furnas and Rauch (1998) studied the use of digital libraries and conclude that in searching for information a 'one-shot query' is very rare. A rather specific or a small group of Digital Libraries (DLs) are addressed by many studies and in development, DLs are seldom addressed. They know how to compare the user experience is essential to be able to compare

DLs. Usability is the major forms of the study, and to contextualize specific DLs user studies and both information behaviour and user experience studies, a more informal approach needs to be followed.

Jones and Cockburn (1996) studied different www browsers in terms of their navigational support. Marshall et al. (1999) studied the use of digital reading devices. Adler et al. (1998) discussed categories of reading to discuss categories of writing concerning the document. These ideas will have an impact on the design of digital libraries as working environments. Allen (1998) discusses user interfaces for different tasks. He found that users with well-developed special abilities were better able to use specially organized query tools than those perception abilities were better developed. This will provide help to design the digital library interfaces. Jones et al. (1999) studied the differences between user interfaces through experimentation. Sugimoto et al. (1997) also followed this approach when comparing five different user interfaces to support access to digital libraries.

Similarly, France et al. (1999) studied the use of digital library user interface by given subjects several tasks. Allen (1998), Bishop (1999), Park (1999) used experimental design for comparing the applicability of user interfaces for digital libraries and Jones and Cockburn (1996) in terms of www browser usability. Several studies (Bishop, 1998; 1999; France et al., 1999; Marshall et al., 1999) employed transaction logs to gain an understanding of the activities users were engaging in with digital libraries. Various data collection techniques have been used to analyze the use of digital libraries. Usability testing technique used by Allen, Bishop, Park and Sugimoto et al. to compare the applicability of user interfaces for digital libraries. Bishop, Covi and Kling relied on interviews to access people's perceptions and use of digital libraries. France et al. Jones et al. Marshall et al. used transaction logs to understand the activities of users within digital libraries. Diary study method was used by Adler et al. and O'Hara et al. Other methods like questionnaire, observation and focus groups were used to understand the usability of systems. User studies are moving into a mature generation by building on earlier foundation research. Wilson (2000) discussed that Action research and Qualitative research are appropriate methodologies for the study of human information behaviour. According to French and Bell (1973), Action research is an integral part of the organisational development consulting process. "Action research aims to contribute both to the practical concerns of people in an immediate problematic situation and the goals of social science by collaboration within a mutually acceptable ethical framework" (Rapaport, 1970: 499). Now Qualitative research is another emerging trend in information science, originated in social science. Under one school of thought, "Qualitative research is the concern with developing concepts rather than applying pre-existing concepts" (Half Penny, 1979) and given the stat of theory in information science, it can well be arranged that 'developing concepts' is what is needed. Qualitative research is suitable to study information-seeking behaviour. These studies reiterate that digital libraries are the focus area of many studies. Several studies have focused on user interfaces and search techniques. But there are fewer studies carried out as compared to studies in the area of hypertext, WWW, lesser extent browsing in digital libraries and information retrieval fields. There is a strong need to focus on the user's requirement of information sources.

Academic libraries have now restored to introduce instructional courses such as library orientation, faculty development programme and bibliographic instructions to stimulating the use of library resources by students. It is more focused on the needs of its users. (Kronick, 1982) Many studies conducted in the field of public libraries. These studies include mostly use studies, behaviour studies etc. of the users of public libraries. A study on library surveys in Australia revealed the social characteristics of public library adult users. This study found that most of the frequent users had a higher standard of education or belong to a higher professional group. The study found a likely increase in public library users except for some disadvantaged groups (Rochester, 1982). In the USA, because of the introduction of media in public libraries, the use of state and local libraries is in an uptrend among better educated and more advanced. (Brown, 1976).

Even in special libraries, the impact of user studies is significant. It helped in understanding the basic requirement and preferences of users of such libraries. This led to networking and computerization in special libraries. They now use consortia on the network as bibliographic centres for interlibrary loan and reference services. (Murphy, 1976)

National Scenario

A significant effort was made by INSDOC (now NISCAIR) and conducted a Use Survey entitled "INSDOC List of Current Scientific Literature" in 1964. After that INSDOC compiled "Indian Science Abstracts". IASLIC conducted a seminar on "User and Library and Information Services", and pay attention towards users. In the year 1967, INSDOC conducted a pilot survey to access the information needs of the researchers of electronics. One pioneer study was conducted by M.S. Sridhar. This study conducted on ISRO Satellite Centre (ISAC), Bangalore. The results of this doctoral work have been published under the title

"Information Behaviour of Scientists and Engineers". The user studies take an exponential growth in recent years. It can be easily found in the literature of library and information science that majority of researches leading to M. Phil. and Ph. D. Degree are conducted on user studies.

1.12. GUIDELINES FOR USER STUDIES

Various pitfalls and limitations of user studies have been indicated here. Essentially they involve expecting too much from the studies and inherent problems in eliciting information from people about an activity to which they attach value judgments. Given these conditions, how can user studies be made most productive for planning policy and programs? The first and essential guideline is to determine at the outset exactly what information is needed. Any library staff contemplating a user study would do well first to define its purposes as precisely as possible. This will determine what data are to be gathered and the size and cost of the investigation. This functional approach will also make clear that the more questions to which answers are sought, the more complex and costly the effort involved. Every question contemplated should be subjected to the rigorous test of whether the information is needed and exactly how it will be used. Once purposes are clear, there is little problem in obtaining responses from library users and even non-users. Properly approached, library patrons respect an effort to learn more about them and their needs, to serve them better. Breaking the ice is more difficult with nonusers, but once they are convinced that a sales gimmick is not involved, most enjoy talking about their reading hopes and habits.

Handled well, a user study can render public relations dividends. This does not mean that all patrons will automatically fill out a questionnaire thrust into their hands. A study lacks reliability if one-half of the forms are found left blank within the library, and this is what occurs if there is no follow-up. What must be done is to check with visitors as they leave; if this is done politely but firmly, returns can usually be obtained from more than 90 per cent of the users.

This rate of return can be achieved if the questionnaire is kept within two pages at most, and to less than ten minutes of response time. Interestingly, if interviews are used instead of questionnaires, library patrons are usually prepared to give more than ten minutes, once they are convinced that a study is designed to improve service; something in the human relationship renders respondents willing to talk for twenty minutes when they may not devote ten minutes to a question form.

In either case, questions should be concrete and immediate-not "How often do you use the library?" but "When was your last visit to the library before today?"; not "What do use the library for?" but "What are you seeking on this visit?" Such questions can be answered more accurately, and are likely to be answered more honestly because people are less disposed to embroider or misrepresent what they are currently doing when the contrary evidence is in full view. Whereas keeping questions specific and immediate may elicit data about non-typical visits on the part of a few users, this is more than counterbalanced by getting hard facts rather than vague hopes. In any case, the returns will be used to establish patterns and not to minister to single individuals. Such inquiries must be done on a sampling basis, both to conserve staff time and to avoid repeated questioning of the same individuals. A week is usually adequate time or two or three different weeks during the year if there are marked variations in use in different seasons. Within the week, some morning, afternoon, evening and weekend hours should be included. It is more important to get as complete returns as possible from all users within the sample hours, rather than extending the study over a longer period simply to accumulate more responses.

One instrument for obtaining data is the short-form questionnaire. It has the advantages of economy and control: specific information can be obtained from a reliable sample of users without excessive time and cost. However, it is circumscribed in scope and depth and should be used only when the purposes of the study are narrow and specific. Another methodology is the interview-in the library for users, in the home for nonusers. This approach is as productive as the interviewer is skilled, and librarians, by definition, should be skilled in getting at individual interests and needs. Interviews are time-consuming, and they pose special problems in getting representative samples. This method suits survey purposes of insight into reader motives and user strategies in acquiring knowledge. It should be used not only for one-time formal studies but as an integral means of continuing client/professional relations.

1.13. STUDIES OF NONUSERS

It stands to reason that a degree of affinity exists between a library and its users. To some extent, the agency is relevant to needs and interests, and to some extent its organization proves usable; otherwise, the users would not be there. Once there, users should be contacted by the librarian and studied as individuals to obtain continuing feedback for appraising and replanning services.

None of this is feasible with nonusers, who constitute well over one-half the community for the public library, and sizable proportions for school and college libraries also. The case can be advanced that if any formal study is to be made, i.e., if the time and money are to be expended, it would best be directed to those who do not come to the library.

Do some people in the service area or service group lack needs and interests for which recorded knowledge is required? How many have such needs or interests but fulfil them to their satisfaction from sources other than the library? Are there some who have tried the library in the past and found it not suitable for their purpose, and if so, why? Are there others with incipient needs and interests who do not know that suitable materials exist, or that the library has them? Few librarians could give even approximate answers to such questions for the community just beyond their doors.

Going into the community at large to seek answers is the

most complex and costly undertaking. Impressions can be gained by contacting individuals by chance and by talking with organized groups, but any valid study involves a random sample of a heterogeneous and dispersed population and involves interviews in some depth. Few sizable communities can be adequately covered with a sample of fewer than 1000 respondents, and interviews by competent agencies currently cost $20 per call, so that the investment required is quite substantial. The sample size can be reduced somewhat by concentrating on one or more subgroups which the library is not reaching-e.g., undereducated adults, avant-garde sophisticated, or top business executives-but even then the task is formidable.

Where studies involving nonusers have been made, the results have had substance and have affected library planning. An example is the Baltimore area, where the series of Deiches studies was based on data from a random sample of 1,913 household^;^' and more recently a survey was made by a government agency12 of information needs of citizens. Findings and recommendations have guided policy-making in the Enoch Pratt Free Library.

Because of the potential value of data about nonusers, and of the considerable technical skill and cost involved, libraries with some similarity in population composition might well combine in commissioning and funding thorough studies. Some library schools, in conjunction with the social research centres of their universities, are competent to carry out such assignments. Another alternative is for the state library agency to commission and finance studies of nonuser groups that characterize several parts of the state. Librarians have come to hold the attitude that scientific research is desirable if carried out by others and paid for by the government. Now that federal funds are more difficult to obtain, individual libraries and state library agencies-if they are seriously concerned about user needs and responses-might well take steps to acquire their planning data. On the statewide level, if this were to be designed not as a one-time cross-section review, but as a periodic series of studies, with some of the same types of information gathered at intervals, the result would be a running record of trends and a much clearer idea of whether efforts to improve service or to meet changed conditions have made a difference. The statistics which states usually acquire annually show expenditures for service provision in the form of money, materials and staff time; user data similarly acquired on a sample basis would show what is accomplished by the investment.

1.14. REVIEW QUESTIONS

1. Elucidate the Concept and meaning of user studies.
2. State the Objectives of user studies.
3. Why Should Conduct User Studies?
4. Illuminate the various methods in conducting user studies.
5. Explain the Recent User Studies in India.
6. Discuss briefly the need for user studies.
7. Explain some of the methodologies/techniques employed for conducting user studies

1.15. BIBLIOGRAPHY

1. ALA World Encyclopedia of Library and Information Science. - Chicago: American Library Association, 1980. p.4 & p.375.
2. Appleton, Leo" Perception of electronic library resources in further education" in " The Electronic Library" vol.24, no.5, 2006. p.619-634 (accessed on 12th March 2008).
3. Ayene, O.C," Self –Efficacy and the students use of electronic resources".- Nigeria, 2000 (accessed on 28th February 2008).
4. Bandura, A" Self-efficacy; The exercise of Control".- New York: Cambridge University Press,1992 (accessed on 2nd May 2008). Bhandari, KM "Information literacy: Nepali Experience" in "INASP Newsletter" no.25, March 2004.
5. Brophy,p "Networking in British Academic Libraries" in "British Journal of Academic librarianship" vol.8, no.1, 1993. p.49-60. Cornwall, Sheila" Academic libraries in the information society" in " New Library World" vol. 96, no.3, 1995. p.35-42.

6. Dermott, Donna" Library instruction for high-risk freshmen" in "Reference Service Review" vol.33, no.4, 2005. p.418-437 (accessed on 28th February 2008).
7. Devarajan G (1989). Users approach in information in libraries Ess New Delhi.
8. Devarajan G (1995) Library and information, user and user studies begin the book, New Delhi.
9. Dr Kaur, Amritpal "Internet and Libraries" in "Library Herald" vol.38, no.1, April-June 2000.
10. Dubey, P.Yogendra "New Challenges in Information Management & E-Learning in the Age of Globalization: Issues and Opportunities" in "Library Hearld" vol.41, no.2, June 2003.
11. Elliot, A "Learning with computers" in "AECA Resource Book Series" vol.3, no.2, p.14-20
12. Mewe H (1972). Reader Instruction in college and university: introductory handbook, Bingley, London.
13. Misra VN, Phadka DN (1988). The user education program at different levels in academic libraries. In:Satyanarayana NR Ed. User education in academic libraries, Ess Ess Publications, New Delhi., p.
14. Pandy SKS (1992). Library and society, Ess New Delhi.Ravi KB (2006). User Education in libraries, Dr Kalia Perumal, library and information science.
15. Pettigrew, K.E., Fidel, R., and Bruce, H. (2001), Conceptual frameworks in information behaviour. Annual Review of Information Science and Technology, 35, 43–78.
16. Rice, R.E., McCreadie, M. and Chang, S.L.(2001), Accessing and Browsing Information and Communication; MIT Press: Cambridge, Mass., 2001.
17. Robinson, M. A. (2010), An empirical analysis of engineers' information behaviours. Journal of the American Society for Information Science and Technology, 61(4), 640–658. Accessed at http://dx.doi.org/10.1002/asi.21290. Accessed on 25th June 2012.
18. Rojas, B.A. (1982), Information systems for the scientific management of agricultural research. Conference on selected issues in agricultural research in Latin America, Madrid, ISNAR.
19. Sahoo, S. K. and Ramesh, D.S (2011), Information seeking behaviour of faculty members of ICFAI business school, Hyderabad. International journal of information dissemination and technology, Oct.-Dec.2011, 1(4), 223-227.

20. Scarrott, G. (1994), Some functions and properties of information, Journal of information science, 20(2), 88-98. Accessed at *http://jis.sagepub.com/*content/20/2/88.full. pdf+html. Accessed on 13th May 2012.
21. Shannon, C and Weaver W (1949), The mathematical theory of Communication, University of Illinois Press, Urbana.

Unit 2

OBJECTIVES
- Sprouting theory of user behaviour
- Analysing the factors influencing the user behaviour
- Limitations in behavioural research
- Aim and objectives of User needs and user education
- Planning of user education
- Problems of user studies and user education.

2.1. INTRODUCTION

"Human being is involved in certain social activities which are complex and interdependent. This phenomenon gives rise to an increasing need for information from some potential sources that are not known to them. Moreover, the needs are myriad, and the variations among people are of difference with regards to context, intellectual level, frequency, and volume of information sources required. Besides these, there are many institutions, organizations, and learned societies, industrial firms, government, and non-government agencies dealing with a variety of information in acquiring and disseminating.

With the growth of information deluge, each one needs information on increasing variety and diversity of level, frequency, volume, and use. This complex situation appears to be ambiguous and heterogeneous so that, information needs of a particular group of users and information flow from a specific situation/organization are difficult to determine. Again, the use of information is so complex that there cannot be a simple system to cope up with the task of effective retrieval without assessing their specific needs. This situation has given rise to the growing concept of information searching and the manner of determining the pattern of searching is said to be considered user behaviour.

Users and their information use studies perhaps form the largest single body of research literature in librarianship. Crawford estimates that well over 1000 user behaviour and information system use studies have appeared in print (Krikelas; 83; p.5). The recent developments in the field have added new dimensions to the research literature. It can be expanded by new approaches to citation studies, automated searching, text-retrieval, and scaling of bibliographical databases. The body of literature on 'user behaviour' within the framework of librarianship is increasing day by day. This incessant growth of various aspects of the subject has led the researchers to concentrate more on service aspects to refine the services or redesign

2.2. INFORMATION

According to Shannon and Weaver (1949) "Information is any stimulus that reduces uncertainty". In the views of Chen and Heron (1982) information is "all knowledge, ideas, facts, data and imaginative works of mind which are communicated formally and/or informally in any format". The information thus covers facts that consist of data, knowledge or wisdom. Facts are the things that are true and known to have happened or already existed. Data is the smallest element of information and represented in any language and any form like a symbol or mathematical signs etc. It also represents people, objects, events and concepts. The knowledge is an organized set of statements of facts or ideas presenting a judgment with some specific reason. It is an experimental result which is transmitted to others through the medium of communication in some form.

In brief, data is a raw fact, whereas information is the statement or product of analysing data to state some facts. Information on a particular area or concept collected together generates knowledge which could be applied in practice. The definition of wisdom is termed as the ability to judge what is true, right lasting or insight (Farlex Free online dictionary). It can also be expressed as an individual quality which comes to one through the acquisition of sound knowledge and also through experience acquired due to age. This trait comprises the ability to see far ahead into the future and select the right alternatives from the available sources. It is the highest form of knowledge which cannot be transferred but can only be acquired. Information is used for decision-making and it is based on data collected and analyzed.

The sources of information are different and grouped into primary sources covering periodicals, research reports, conference proceedings, patents, standards, thesis, trade literature etc. which provides nascent primary and firsthand information to the user community. Whereas secondary sources cover compilation of published information through primary sources and consist of indexing and abstracting periodicals, reviews, trends or progress reports, annuals, handbooks, encyclopedias, dictionaries, textbooks etc. the tertiary sources are in the form of yearbooks, directories, biographies, guides to literature, lists of research in progress etc. which are useful for the users. Information is made available to the society through various sources and forms (print or non-print/digital). Information need from the view of information science is a vague awareness of something missing and as culminating in locating the information that contributes to understanding the meaning (Kuhlthau 1993). It is also described as Analogues State of Knowledge (ASK) (Belkin et. al. 1982) or a gap in an individual's knowledge in sense-making situations (Dervin and Nilan 1986). Information is regarded as wealth and everyone needs it for different purposes. The pinpointed information helps users to build the castle of advanced knowledge. Information is very useful for decision making in any field and at all the levels.

2.3. INFORMATION PROPERTIES

Information is used by everyone with specific application and has distinctive properties (Scarrott 1994) like:
- Information is not consumed due to usage but it generates new and innovative concepts. It can be shared simultaneously without any loss of information
- It is a democratic resource which can be consumed and is required by both rich and poor, literate or illiterate.
- Information is dynamic, ever-growing, expanding and continuing. Information can be the difference you perceive in your environment or within yourself. (Case 2002).

It is concluded that information is vital and needed by everyone to contribute to knowledge. Every human being is in search of information for various purposes.

2.4. INFORMATION: NEED

The concept of the term "information need" has been coined by Robert Taylor (1962) an American information scientist (Dave 2012), whereas Brittain (1970) expressed the meaning of need as "need expressed by the user or need which user cannot express or immediate need or future or deferred or potential need etc." In short, the need is simply defined as what user requires for his work, it may be for research, education, or updating knowledge or any other definite purpose. "An information need is a recognition that your knowledge is inadequate to satisfy a goal that you have" Case (2002). Thus, information is any fact needed to take decision or fulfilment of need. Information need forces user to seek information. The need for information is continuous for users and is needed to keep the users aware of new or latest developments in the field of interest, analyse the state of the art of the topic etc. The information has value and is needed by everyone as per the requirements of the task.

2.5. INFORMATION: TYPES AND QUALITIES

According to Shera, there are six types of information:

1. Conceptual information : It relates to ideas, theories and hypothesis about the relationship which exists among the variables in an area.

2. Empirical information : It relates to data and experience of research which may be drawn from oneself or communicated through others.

3. Procedural information : This is the data which is obtained, then manipulated and tested through investigation.

4. Stimulatory information : It is motivated by oneself or the environment.

5. Policy information : It is focused on the decision making process.

6. Directive information : It is used for co-coordinating and enabling effective group activity.

The qualities of information as listed by Rojas (1982) are accessibility, comprehensiveness, precision, compatibility, timeliness, clarity, flexibility, verifiability, fair and quantifiable etc. Thus, information is comprehensive, which can be used and accessed for generating new knowledge. Precise, accurate, and competitive information is required by researchers or users of the information.

2.6. INFORMATION: EXPLOSION AND INFORMATION OVERLOAD

The knowledge society is using information and generating new knowledge. The information explosion is so high that information is doubling within a couple of years and becoming difficult to manage and is the main cause for information overload which is witnessed in the knowledge society. In addition to this, the usage of information technology in publishing information has added more load on the users. Jungwirth (2002) rightly indicated that nearly 1000 books are published internationally every day and printed statistics indicated by him shows that printed knowledge is doubled every five years. Due to digital publications, the growth rate is being reduced to a few years. Information overload is generally considered as a situation in which an individual's efficiency in using the information in his work is hampered by the amount of relevant and potentially useful information available to him. Information technology is considered to be a major cause of information overload. The information explosion and use of ICT have made the situation of users more complicated and complex for searching and getting desired information. The information-seeking habits of users have changed and puzzled them due to unawareness of proper information sources and methods of extraction of data. Information users need training for searching for proper information from e-resources.

2.7. INFORMATION-SEEKING BEHAVIOUR

A librarian's major task is to satisfy the users. To undertake such a critical task that involves a clear understanding of the psychological, physiological, and social factors of human nature/beings, one has to develop a deep understanding of user-librarian interaction based on human behaviour, which often remains unpredictable and complex. If one looks deeper into the information sphere, the understanding of human involvement is more a factor that contributes to the existence of the system. In that, the attribute, personality, and motivational structures that constitute the overall 'behaviour' of the human being are seen. A person needing information develops certain behavioural options. There are five main classes of these options: (1) to wait; (2) to act; (3) to generate information; (4) to seek information; (5) to opt-out of the situation (Christie; 1981; p.150). Each of these classes can be broken down into fixed groups and eventually into the specific concrete options available at a given point in time. But the general classes apply at all points of the behaviour structure. The user can wait before deciding what to do, can act on the information retrieved so far, can generate information, can seek information, or can opt-out of the situation, if the same does/does not suit his taste or need.

The human brain acts as a processor of information. Zweizig in his work utilized the model of the individual as an information processor. Bell's (1991; p.8) study analyses many information-processing mechanisms in animals which apply to human being and provides a foundation for understanding searching strategies and tactics, patterns of resource distribution, and a trade-off between competition and risk on time minimization and energy maximization. Charge and Rice

(1993; p.250) have further clarified Bell's model of ecology influencing animals' searching behaviour providing some insights for the development of human behaviour theories.

Researchers in communication and psychology have shifted their move to view 'persons' as active and purposeful assets. As a result, human cognition and behaviour have become increasingly a matter to be discussed and applied as a mechanism for information processing, social and cognitive psychologists have developed many common concerns within this type of information - processing framework regarding such issues as the nature of the cognitive structure, verbal memory, the processing of movies and visual information, impression formation, and stereotyping (Sypher and Applegate; 1984; p.310). However, information is not only an element of learning but also is a set of stimuli for those human beings who consider it as the sustenance of their sound existence. For those who like learning and knowledge, their attitude to information is equally electrifying their activities. Descartes has argued that only some human action stemmed from material and mechanical sources and information being the most vibrant material develops certain behavioural patterns in the human mind for a concrete action to be undertaken. Hence, the need for information and its seeking pattern is a genuine characteristic.

2.7.1. Information-Seeking Behaviour: Definition

The phrase 'Information Seeking Behaviour' has been defined variously by different authors. The following definitions of information-seeking behaviour will, however, make the concept clearer. According to Krikelas (1983), information-seeking behaviour refers to "any activity of an individual that is undertaken to identify a message that satisfies a perceived need".

King defined information-seeking behaviour "as a manner in which a user conducts Himself with a given information environment. It is, therefore, regarded as essentially, a process of interaction between the user and the rest of the information system (Manda, 1991; p. 18). The act of searching or finding information can be ascribed to information seeking. Such an activity begins when the user perceives that the existing knowledge is less than that needed to deal with some problem(s). With the end of that perception, the process of seeking ends. Developing an instinct for information is a sort of behaviour and the process of searching the same is considered as Information Seeking Behaviour. One can ask 'what is the basis of seeking'? Seeking arises when there is some perceived need. It is required to determine why individuals selectively seek certain kinds of information while they ignore or reject others. Based on Festinger's cognitive dissonance theory, it was suggested that individuals seek information that confines their pre-existing opinions, attitudes, and favours their predisposition (Rahim; 1990; p.100). In this same framework, it is noted that individual's information-seeking behaviour is not guided by the relative importance of relevance of an issue, but rather by their pre-existing attitudes towards the issue. On the other hand, Hawking and Daly (1988; p.202) have added the selectivity process of dissonance theory. They have viewed that the selectivity process is not only a cognitive phenomenon, but it should be viewed interactively with other variables such as emotions, availability of information, and a specific domain of information. The work of Donohew et. al. (1990; p. ll), 'knowledge gap' contended that what motivates individuals to seek information is the relevance of such information to individual situations. Persons having higher social status or educational attainments are better equipped with information, but those who obtain from information seeking environments are seldom considered the least knowledgeable.

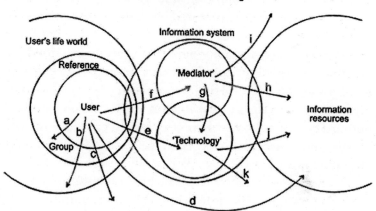

Fig. 2.1. Three fold view of information seeking

The above figure suggests a threefold view of information seeking: the context of the seeker, the 'system' employed, and the information resources that might be drawn upon. All of this is shown to exist within a 'universe of knowledge' that might be drawn upon directly by the information seeker or the intermediary, though, for example, persons as embodiments of knowledge. Note that 'technology' was interpreted widely, in the general sense of anything that aids action: at the time, the application of information technology to information seeking was in its infancy, and neither the personal computer nor the World Wide Web existed. One of the strengths of the model is that, despite the changes that have occurred, it continues to serve as a valid framework.

2.8. HISTORY OF INFORMATION BEHAVIOUR RESEARCH

Information seeking behaviour of human being is as old as his searching ability. Everyone knows that when he was living in the natural circumstances he was spent maximum time in the food search. For that, he thinks and creates new ideas, according to his previous experiences. He collects information from his soundings and uses it. It was the first and informal as well as unstructured behaviour for information seeking. As per the contemporary situation, it is much interested to see his formal, well-structured attempts towards information seeking. In 1930 the University of Chicago awarded a first doctoral degree in Library science. Various reputed social science researchers, Douglas Waples and Bernard Berelson showed their skills to this respective subject. Waples published abstracts of results from dozens of studies on public library use. From 1948 to 1959 there were several conferences organized on scientific information. Their major attention was on, how much money has been invested in scientific research, and how many scientists gathered and used information for their research work. Two major publications have published concerns about this matter named "21-Report Series." And "Project on Scientific Information Exchange in Psychology (American Psychology Association). More recently, however, some researchers came to feel that "information seeking" suggested only explicit efforts to locate information, and did not include the many other ways people and information interacted. In the 1990s, the term "information behaviour" came into wide use to replace "information seeking." the old Guard objected that the phrase is a non-sequitur – information does not "behave"- but they lost out, and "information behaviour" remains the most commonly used today (Marcia Bates, 2010). During the 1960s in the United States have a lot of funds were available for social science research. It motivated researchers to develop large, well-designed studies regarding the social aspects of scientific communication and information use. As part of this culture, many important studies also came into existence on information use and library use by the general public. During the 1960s and 1970s, some practices have been done on identity politics of race, gender, sexual orientation, and the economically underprivileged groups. These studies indirectly played a considerable role in the direction of information seeking research studies. In the late sixth and early seventh decade of the 20th-century information, the behaviour has been included as a research area of library and information science education policy in the North American countries. It was as similar as a platform for scientists in their discipline. In 1973 a national conference was held on, "information service needs of the nation", by the national commission on libraries and information science (Marcia Bates 2010). During the 7th decade, the focus on social science has much turned from natural sciences. Not the only United States but Britain has put much concentration on social science research. Both countries have allocated grants for it. This situation helped to promote the research in information seeking Behavior. In the 80s and 90s many institutions such as, "The J. Paul Getty Trust" have put their interest in this regard. They released grants for the research in the respective area. In the 2000s, Kari and Hartel (2007) studied the information behaviour of people involved in activities with the aim of fulfilment and self-realization, and their research provided examples of what could be learned along this line (Marcia Bates 2010). Over the decades, varying amounts of information behaviour research has been done in various professional contexts as well, including the health sciences. Law, and business, Among the professions, it is almost certainly the health sciences where the largest body of information behaviour research has been done- probably due to abundant funding- while the education profession despite the importance of information seeking for teachers, seems, mysteriously, to have drawn very little attention.

2.9. FACTORS OF MOTIVATION IN INFORMATION SEEKING

There is a varying degree of motivation to seek information. It primarily depends upon the work situations or level of requirements or organizational factors. Individuals with this motivation to seek information on politics may not have the same degree of interest to seek information on scientific research/ or on investigative journalism. Gold Haber et. al. (1978; p. 82) suggest that persons are interested to seek information concerning their work environment. The motivation to seek information lies in the information itself. Persons seeking information about job-related matters are very often motivated by the desire to get rewards for successful performance. Individuals will not be motivated to seek such information because the same is perceived, that being reinforced.

Individuals' referent criterion or experience also contributes to their information-seeking behaviour. The presence of a referent criterion would reduce the degree of probability of individuals seeking information because the need for new information is minimised. (Grunig and Dibrows; 1977; p. 145-67). They contend that the stronger the involvement, the higher the probability that individuals would seek information about the situation In a study of a health information system; Etteme et al (1983; p.525) find that circumstantial factors as predictors of information seeking would not be powerful enough to generate the active search for information when such information is not readily available. In situations where information related to the specific issue is readily available, individual situational factors would again emerge as a better predictor of information seeking.

Individuals with time may exhibit different information-seeking behaviour because of a significant difference like the problem. Certain jobs and lifestyles may be characterized by the degree of constraints they happen to face. There can be two types of situations in which information is consulted: (1) continuous and (2) discrete. Bureaucrats, for example, while dealing with specific issues face discrete problems. But journalists whose responsibility is to report in a daily manner need information continuously. The distinction is in the predominant nature, and this predominance may manifest itself in a general pattern of information-seeking. How the users, especially, scholars use the resources and that is their habit of seeking information has been the concern of information intermediary. The same is being studied from a variety of perspectives. It is the responsibility of not only library and information science but also sociology, psychology, and cognitive science, and communication studies. Increasingly, ethnography documenting the behaviour of individual scholars in their teaching and research environments will provide needed context for such work. Limited progress in explaining and predicting human information seeking, retrieval, and use, however, may be attributed to a lack of agreement about whether the appropriate goal is to develop general or restrict investigations to descriptions of specific cases. (Sandstorm; 1971; p.418).

There are different dimensions of behavioural assessment, while some emphasise the sociological approach as the appropriate one, others prefer psychology or cognitive science that leads the behavioural patterns. Some still say the communication system to be the mainstay in shaping the behavioural designs while others consider observable behaviour or actions of the information user that mould the human information-seeking behaviour.

2.10. CLASSIFICATION OF USER STUDIES

A user study is a technique to assess the pattern of using library resources. By this, the researcher can be able to examine and discover certain other factors associated with the use of resources. The classification of user studies differs from author to author, since there are no fixed principles concerning taxonomical divisions of such user studies. According to Prasad (1992), Menial has classified the user studies under three broad groups such as:

(a)   Studies dealing with User behaviour;
(b)   Studies dealing with the Information Use; and

(c) Studies dealing with Information-flow".

Similarly, R.G Prasher (1991) has classified the user studies under four broad categories such as (a) descriptive studies, (b) analytical studies, (c) survey-based studies, and (d) user-based studies. He has classified such studies taking into account the types of explanations provided in the studies. The different classes of User studies are discussed below:

(a) Studies dealing with the Behaviour of the Users : Such type of user studies primarily denotes a method of identifying the behavioural pattern of the users. It means such user studies are designed to reflect the information-seeking behaviour of the users in a given library environment. In such type, the interaction of the user is more a factor that is verified and determined while identifying the attitudes and behaviour of users towards the library system and its' valuable learning resources.

(b) Studies dealing with the Information Use : In this case, the pattern of using literature by the users becomes the basis of the study which can give a deep insight into information handling and building a collection development for libraries as well as provide the information services more effectively. In other words, any user study which is conducted to find out the use of any communication medium falls under the ambience of this category of user studies.

(c) Studies dealing with Information Need : Now-a-days, in Library and Information Science field the concept of information, information needs and information flow which are confined to users, form one of the most extensive and amorphous areas of research. Such type of user studies is primarily designed to find out the pattern of library use, information systems, library materials, information seeking and gathering habits of various groups of users, etc. to elicit a substantial amount of valuable input for effective library planning.

2.11. THE ELEMENT OF INFORMATION SEEKING BEHAVIOUR

Information-seeking is a matter more or less related to the sense-making in which the individual chooses an item of information that best fits his needs and purposes. Making an in-depth study on 'information needs' Dervin and Nilan (1986; p.12) have proposed a paradigm shift for information-seeking behaviour. They have identified an automotive set of premises and assumptions, the essence of an alternative paradigm in a set of six elements. They are:

1. The conception of information as objective versus subjective;
2. Information users as passive recipient or objective information versus purposive, self-controlling, sense-making beings;
3. The user of information on behaviour applied across situations versus behaviour understood as the result of the dialogue between system and user in which need articulation goes through situationally bound interactions;
4. The study of user behaviour primarily in the context of user interaction with the system versus holistic approaches that focus on the whole social interaction;
5. Focus on external behaviour versus internal cognition; and
6. Concerns that a focus on individual behaviour yields too much variation for systems to integrate versus the need, with individuality in user behaviour. They, however, conclude that traditional approaches have aspired to sophisticated quantitative techniques... yet in the context of the impetus of the paradigm shifts, scholars are now calling for supplementing quantitative approaches with inductive, qualitative approaches (ibid; p. 16).

2.12. METHODS TO FIND OUT THE INFORMATION-SEEKING BEHAVIOUR OF USERS

Different users possess different information needs to find out their information needs and information-seeking methods user studies, user survey, studies on collection use and community studies are very helpful User study comprises a study of people's need for, and use of information.

A user study may be defined as a systematic study of information requirements of users m order to facilitate meaningful exchange between the information systems and users. There is a need to study user because

1. User attitudes are essential considerations in the design of library services
2. Users have ways of doing things and there should be accommodated in the design of services
3. Users have a way of doing things that should be changed

For finding out the information-seeking attitude of users the following questions may be asked

1. What do users require from the library, in terms of type, quality, and range of services to satisfy their needs?
2. What does the user do about his/her need?
3. How does the user select available resources?
4. How does the user search for information?

The reasons for conducting the user studies are

1. To identify the actual strengths and weakness of the library
2. To identify the levels and kinds of user needs
3. To identify faculty and student priorities for library resources and services
4. To identify the limitations or problems which seem to discourage the use of the library
5. To identify the level of involvement or participation of

faculty and students and the library programme
6. To improve the organization and planning for library services at both the local and national level

The user study on a particular day reveals to how many readers used what service and perhaps that the amount of such use varied according to some external characteristics such as interest or status within an organization These facts do not illustrate such materials as need, nor do they give much assistance on planning future systems and services of more use are the studies of people's information needs and information-seeking behaviour, particularly where there are based on what happens rather than on people's opinions of what might happen of primary interest are those studies which contribute to the understanding of the user. Several methods of evaluating the user, user studies have gamed significance as a well - established measurement technique, although methodologies employed are varied. "They are a systematic in-depth attempt to obtain an objective view of a facility and match it against certain standards of efficiency, service or rate of improvement" The students and faculty are the users of the library, towards whom all services are directed Their attitude reflects the extent to which the efforts of librarians are successful m developing the resources and services of the library to meet their needs User surveys means surveying the user by using questionnaires, the interview method and of a random sample of users and non-users Information about user needs to be collected through observation and informal interaction with the user is more authentic to understand their needs and behaviour This will explain their area of interest and their needed books

2.13. MODELS OF INFORMATION SEEKING BEHAVIOUR

Most of the information-seeking behaviour models are of variety: they are statements that attempt to describe an information-seeking activity, the causes, and consequences of that activity, or the relationships among stages in information-seeking behaviour. Very few models do search advance to the stage of specifying relationships among theoretical propositions, rather, they are at a pre-theoretical stage, but may suggest relationships that might be fruitful to explore or test. Models of information behaviour, however, appear to be fewer than those devoted to information-seeking behaviour or information searching. The models have been discussed one by one.

(a) Wilson's Model of Information Behaviour: Wilson proposed his original concept of information behaviour in the form of three models, representing a way of thinking about the field of person-centric studies. The most cited model from his original concept focuses on the origin of information needs and barriers to seeking information (Wilson, 2005). The model states that the interplay between (a) personal primary needs (e.g., physiological needs, affective needs, and cognitive needs), (b) person's social role (e.g., work-related responsibilities and performance expectations from the individual), and (c) external environmental factors (e.g., work environment, socio-cultural environment, politico-economic environment, and physical environment) makes the person realize about their information needs. As a result, the person attempts to seek information by overcoming personal, interpersonal, and environmental barriers

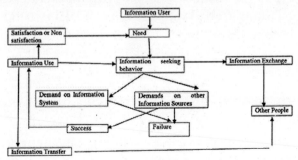

Fig. 2.2. Wilson's Model of Information Behaviour (1981)

Wilson suggests that information-seeking behaviour arises due to the need perceived by an information user in different stages or sequences. To satisfy that need, the user makes demands upon formal or informal information sources or services. These demands for information result in success or failure to find relevant information. If the result becomes successful, the individual then makes use of the information found and may either fully or partially satisfy the perceived need or indeed. The model also highlights that part of the information-seeking behaviour may involve other people through information exchange and that information perceived as useful may be passed to other people, as well as being used or instead of being used by the person himself or herself.

The second model states that any need perceived by the person prompts them to seek information. The model identifies basic needs in the form of physiological, cognitive, and affective needs. Importantly, the needs and barriers to pursuing the needs arise in the same context which may be a combination of personal characteristics, a person's role at work or in life, and the environments (political, economic, technological, etc.). A person may demand information from formal or informal information sources, services, and systems (e.g., libraries, online databases, community centres, etc.) to satisfy information needs. In the case of a successful attempt, the person uses the information to satisfy their information need fully or partially. Reiteration of the search process is possible (Wilson, 1981). The model also depicts that the person may involve others for exchanging and using information, which indicates the element of reciprocity, a characteristic feature of human interactions (Wilson, 2006).

(b) Wilson's Model of Information Behaviour (1996) : The third model suggests a three-fold view of information seeking. The context of the seeker, i.e., the overall life of the person, the system employed (e.g., computer or machine-based system used directly or with the help of a mediator), and the information resources (e.g., print or digital) form the three components of the model. Technology represents any set of devices, tools, or mechanism that aids information-seeking behaviour. The model underlines the dynamic nature of information seeking and presents it as an ongoing process. The primary structure of Wilson's 1996 model is based on his first one. Here the 'intervening variables' that fall under the third group in the picture show how the information-seeking barriers evolve during the needs of information. These are psychological, demographic, role-related or interpersonal, environmental, and source characteristics. The 1996 model now also identifies 'information-seeking behaviour' (the fifth group of concepts in the figure), namely passive attention, passive search, active search, and on-going search.

The three models filled in a significant research gap in the information science literature. They became of quick interest for scholars in information systems, consumer behaviour, health sciences, and other fields. However, they were not generalizable enough for various user groups to capture their contextual factors that affect information behaviour. Hence, Wilson proposed the revised model of information behaviour in 1996, which integrated studies from decision-making,

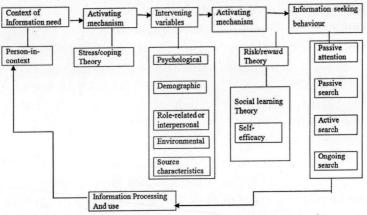

Fig. 2.3. Wilson's Model of Information Behaviour (1996)

psychology, innovation, health communication, and consumer research. General systems theory and phenomenology influenced the construction of the revised model (Wilson, 2005).

(c) Dervin's Model: Dervin's sense-making theory has developed over several years, and cannot be seen simply as a model of information-seeking behaviour. She indicates this theory as a set of assumptions, a theoretic perspective, a methodological approach, a set of research methods, and a practice' designed to cope with information perceived as a human tool designed for making sense of a reality assumed to be both chaotic and orderly. However, sense-making is implemented in terms of four constituent elements - a situation in which information problems arise; a gap, which identifies the difference between the contextual situation and the desired situation an outcome, that is, the consequences of the sense-making process, and a bridge, that is, some means of closing the gap between situation and outcome. To bridge this gap, individuals seek information to make new sense and use this information to help them in everyday life. The outcome represents the use of information to complete a task. This makes the sense-making experience a holistic experience Situation Gap. Dervin presents these elements in terms of triangle factor: situation, gap/bridge, and outcome, which is represented in figure 3.

Fig. 2.4. Dervin's 'sense-making' triangle

However, it may be preferable to use the bridge metaphor more directly and present the model in Fig.4 as below. The central activities of sense-making are information-seeking, processing, creating, and using. By using the Sense-making approach to study users' information behaviour, researchers can discover people's strategies, expectations, attitudes, and anxieties within their lives and work situations (Solomon 1997).

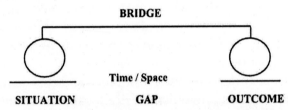

Fig. 2.5. Dervin's sense-making model re-drawn

Sense-making provides a theoretical perspective on information needs, but it is also a methodological approach that could be used to study information usage behaviour.

(d) Cheuk Wai -Yi's Information-Seeking and Using Process Model: Cheuk Wai-Yi's information-seeking and use (ISU) process model is based on Dervin's Sense-making approach. The model was tested on different professional user groups. Cheuk Wai-Yi developed the ISU process model to illustrate the dynamic and diverse information-seeking behaviour exhibited by each "individual-in-situation". The model states that "human information-seeking and using behaviour" create the situations that prompt the information need. The ISU Process model is made up of the following crucially different situations and information-seeking aspects that form the framework for the identification of information behaviour associated with each ISU situation. The seven situations are task initiating; focus forming; ideas assuming; ideas confirming; ideas rejecting; ideas finalising; and the passing on of ideas. The information-seeking aspects are the use and choice of information sources, information relevance judgement criteria, information organisation and information presentation strategies, feelings, and definition of information. Cheuk Wai-Yi finds in his theory a relationship between the above mentioned seven situations and information-seeking aspects. The model establishes that people move between the seven ISU situations in multidirectional paths. Cheuk Wai-Yi contends that this makes the process of human information seeking and use systematic and predictable. Cheuk Wai-Yi also determined that although people-belonging-to-the-same professional-group" use similar information sources and channels they do not have the same information needs.

(e) Norman's Cognitive Model of Information Seeking: A cognitive account of the standard model derived from Norman's influential model of general task performance (Norman, 1988, Hearst 2009) is presented below. The model given by Norman depicts a broad perspective on how people operate in the world. According to his model, a person must first have a basic idea of what they want and the goals they want to achieve. Then they mentally prepare their model of the situation and decide on some kind of action to be taken which will affect them, other related people or objects to achieve their goal.

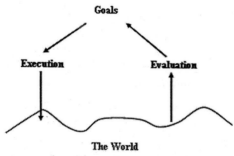

Fig. 2.6. Norman's Cognitive Execution-Evaluation Model

Norman divided actions into actual doing (execution) and then checking (evaluation) the results. After taking an action, a person must assess what kind of change occurred and if there were any changes, and whether these changes had a positive impact on achieving the desired goals. Norman also suggested that the less knowledge a person has about their task, the less they might be successful in formulating goals and assess results. Recognizing a need for information is akin to formulating and becoming conscious of a goal. Formulating the problem and expressing the information need through queries or navigation in a search system corresponds to executing actions. The examination of the results to determine whether the information need is satisfied corresponds to the evaluation part of the model. Query reformulation is needed if the distance between the goal and the state of the world is too large.

(f) Foster's Non-Linear ISB Model: Foster's non-linear model of information-seeking behaviour represents a shift towards a new understanding of this subject area. The model is based on findings of an interview-based naturalistic inquiry on the information-seeking behaviour of a sample of 45 academics and postgraduate researchers representing many disciplines (Foster 2004). It comprises three core processes like Opening, Orientation, and Consolidation in addition to three levels of contextual interaction: Cognitive, Internal, and External. The process of "Opening" includes breadth exploration, networking, keyword searching, browsing, monitoring, chaining, and serendipity, as shown below. The "Orientation" process consists of defining a problem, building a picture, and identifying the shape of existing research. "Consolidation" refers to the process of having enough knowledge, redefining, and incorporating the same. It is also the stage of verifying and finishing the task.

According to Foster the model's external influences are categorized as social and organizational also covering the time, the project, and accessibility of resources. Foster also found the social networking aspect of the interdisciplinary experience to be one of the most significant factors influencing access to information resources. The internal influences refer to prior

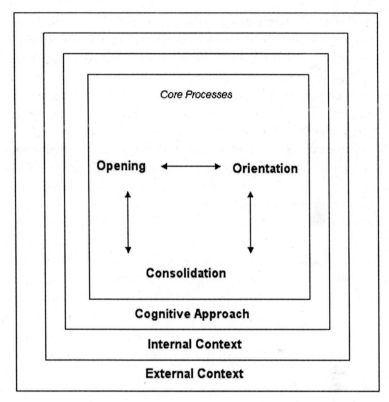

Fig. 2.7. Foster's Non-Linear ISB Model

knowledge on the part of the information seeker, in addition to self-perception and self-efficacy. The cognitive approach describes the participants' willingness to identify and use information that might be relevant to an interdisciplinary problem. One practical implication of the model is that it suggests a need to revise the teaching of information literacy and library skills, with a move towards a holistic skill programme, including curriculum development and training design. The new model offers a base of the framework for educators and library professionals to teach academic and non-academic, expert and non-expert information users in a manner that reflects actual behaviours' and real-world solutions rather than the artificial conceptualization of stages. Foster's presentation of information-seeking behaviour as a "dynamic holistic process" and its insightful implications for teaching information skills also indicated that further research is planned to make the study suitable for generalization by adopting a mixed methodology, incorporating both quantitative and qualitative approaches (Foster 2004). Apart from these models Dave (2012) listed out few more ISB models in his study like the Episodic Model developed by Belkin. This model is based on intuition and insight and concentrates on four dimensions like the method of interaction (Searching), the goal of interaction (Selecting), Mode of retrieval (recognition), and Resource consideration. The information foraging model was defined by Stuart Card and others and is based on thinking that information seekers use clues from summaries, images, and links to get information. Elfreda Chatman developed a model "Life in the round Model" and she explained the fact that unless an initial problem arises, there is no point in seeking information. From the review of the above ISB models, it could be deduced that all the ISB models have similarities except few elaborated points.

(g) Blom's Task Performance Model : A study of the factors that influence the information needs and information-seeking behaviour of consulting engineers within the contexts of problem-solving and decision-making in work situations can also be illuminated by studying Blom's Task Performance model. Blom's (1983) Task Performance Model is based on Blom's research into scientists' information needs and its use. The theory is based on the following hypothesis:

- an information service aims to contribute to the successful task performance of the potential users of such a service.
- *information* is input to problem-solving, decision making, planning, any planned activity, or to the increase of knowledge.

- information needs or task performance needs are the requirements for information to fulfil a certain task.
- the following factors are in interaction with each other:
- the purpose, problem area, and methods of the scientific discipline
- environmental factors, especially in an employing organisation
- the personal attributes of the scientist.

This means that the demands placed on an information service are given precedence over the demands of the user. Figure 2.7 shows that the task of the scientist is always performed within the context of the scientific discipline; the environment; and the scientist as an individual. The different

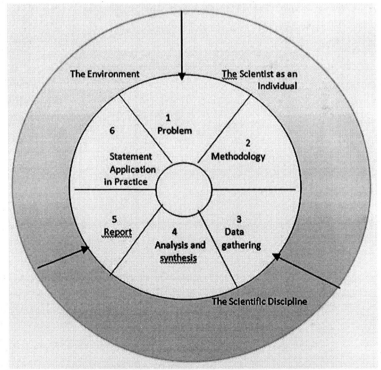

Fig. 2.8. Blom's scientific communication system

steps involved in the research process as illustrated in Blom's model are the problem statement, methodology, data gathering, analysis and synthesis, report, and application in practice. These steps can be equated with the steps in the information process. The most important environmental factors influencing the task performance of the scientist and his information needs are those concerned with the employing organization. Another important influence on the mutual exchange of information is interpersonal relations and social intercourse, as well as patterns of friendship within the organization

(h) Leckie Et Al's Model of the Information-Seeking of Professionals: According to Leckie et al, this model is general, the research scholar decided to group the model with task performance and task-based models in work-related contexts. Leckie et al focused on how the professional's work roles and tasks influence his or her information-seeking behaviour. The study was conducted to examine the information-seeking behaviour of librarians, academics, researchers, doctors, nurses, engineers, lawyers, and many others. She notes that these studies examine how information practices embedded within professional work, how those information-related practices function to contribute to the professional's work, and whether or not those practices can be improved or changed for the better.

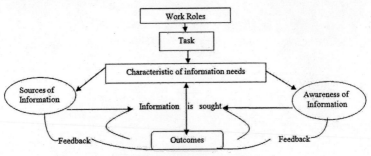

Fig. 2.9. Leckie Et Al's model

The six components of Leckie et al's model are interrelated and dependent on each other. The components are as follows:

(i) Work roles and associated tasks: Professionals lead complicated work lives because they have to play a multiplicity of roles in the course of their daily work, such as service provider, administrator or manager, researcher, educator, and student. Leckie found that different jobs have to be performed by a single professional. For example, engineers are involved both in an operational unit as well as supervisory responsibility for those who operate the unit. The impact on the roles undertaken by engineers could have a bearing on the types of information required and how such information is sought and used.

Factors influencing information needs: Information needs arise when a person assigns to a specific task that is associated with one or more of the work roles played by the professional. Leckie had found that the information needs of the engineer are determined or characterized by their context, frequency, predictability, importance, and complexity, age, profession, specialization, career stage, and geographic location.

Factors affecting information-seeking: Leckie et al. (1996) clarified various factors that affect information-seeking behaviour. These factors involve the sources of information, and awareness of information, and the outcomes of the information-seeking process.

(j) Kuhlthau's Information Search Process: Kuhlthau's information search process (ISP) model in 1991 focuses on two aspects: affective and cognitive during the process of information searching. This ISP of Kuhlthau is a six-stage process of information-seeking behaviour in library and information science. Kuhlthau identified the following stages in the information-seeking process:

- task initiation: uncertainty;
- topic selection: confusion, sometimes anxiety;
- pre-focus exploration: confusion, frustration, sometimes threat and doubt;
- focus formation: optimism, the confidence of ability to complete the task;
- information collection: realization of extensive work to be done, direction, confidence;
- presentation: relief, sometimes satisfaction and dissatisfaction.

Kuhlthau characterized the first stage, initiation as the stage when a person becomes aware that information will be needed to "complete an assignment". This stage of the information-seeking process is filled with feelings of apprehension and uncertainty. In the next stage, selection where a person has chosen an idea, topic, or problem to proceed. At this point, the person is now less uncertain and feels a sense of optimism and a readiness to start the information search process. The third stage, the exploration process, is when students or information seekers become confused when they encounter "inconsistent or incompatible" information. It is at this point that information seeker may become discouraged, express feelings of doubt, and plan of abandoning their search process. Kuhlthau considers this stage as the most difficult stage. The fourth stage namely focus formulation, which is considered as the key point, states that a focused perspective is formed, and uncertainty gradually decreases, and clarity is achieved. The information seeker starts to evaluate the gathering information. At this point, a focused perspective begins to form and there is not as much confusion and uncertainty as in earlier stages Formulation is considered to be the most important stage of the process. The information seeker will here formulate a personalized construction of the topic from the general information gathered in the exploration phase. The fifth stage, a collection where the information seeker gathers the information which is relevant to the topic. At this point, the information seeker understands the direction; he or she must have confidence. Consequently, his/her uncertainty diminishes and becomes interested and deeply involved in the search process. At this point, confidence grows in the search process. In the sixth stage, presentation is when the individual has completed the information search and information seekers prepare to present or use their findings that were found through the process. They experience relief and a sense of satisfaction if the search process is successful or disappointed if they feel that the search was a failure. Kuhlthau states that these stages of the ISP encompass three aspects - "the affective" i.e. feelings, the cognitive, i.e. thoughts, the physical, i.e. actions.

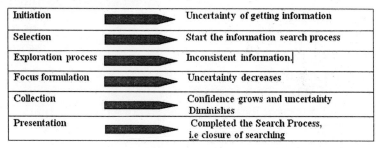

Fig. 2.10. Kuhlthau's six stages Information Search Process

(k) Ellis's Behavioural Model of Information Searching Strategies : Ellis studied the activities and perceptions of social science scholars consisting of psychologists, educationalists, economists, sociologists, historians, geographers, and political scientists at the University of Sheffield of the United Kingdom. From the results, Ellis identified 6 major categories to cover the characteristics of the information-seeking patterns of social scientists, namely

1. Starting,
2. Chaining,

3. Browsing
4. Differentiating,
5. Monitoring, and
6. Extracting.

According to Ellis, starting refers to seeking information on a new topic and gathering initial relevant information. Starting includes activities that form the initial search for information. These could be familiar sources used before or less familiar sources that can provide relevant information. These initial sources can lead to additional sources or references. Following up on these new leads from an initial source is the activity of Chaining. Chaining, as referred by Ellis, refers to the following references in a work to its cited works (backward) and finding new citations to this work (forward). Backward chaining occurs when pointers or references from an initial source are followed, while forward chaining identifies and follows up on other sources that refer to an initial source or document. The next category, according to Ellis is browsing in which the individual often simplifies browsing by looking through tables of contents, lists of titles, subject headings, names of organizations or persons, abstracts and summaries, and so on. Browsing takes place in many Browsing involves looking through tables of contents, lists of titles, subject headings, names of organizations or persons, abstracts, and summaries of the required topic. Next stage after browsing is differentiating, where the information seeker filters and selects from among the sources by taking note of the differences between the nature and quality of the information offered. In this situation, the information seeker can judge whether the information is ready to fulfil his/her needs. Monitoring, as described by Ellis is the process of keeping abreast of knowledge about the latest developments in areas of research interests. By monitoring, the information seeker concentrates on core sources of information which may include personal contacts and publications. Extracting is the process an information seeker can achieve extracting by directly consulting the source, or by indirectly looking through bibliographies, indexes, or online databases. So in this sequence, the information-seeking process is supposed to be ended. Two other categories are identified by Ellis, namely; Verifying which is checking the accuracy of the information, and Ending which may refer to as 'tying up loose ends' through a final search are also identified.

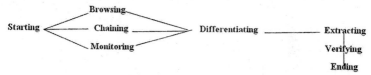

Fig. 2.11. Ellis's Model of Behaviour

Ending: Ellis's model is not only applicable to academics and researchers but also the categories may apply to other groups of users as well.

1. Choo's Behavioural Model of Information-Seeking on the Web: Choo et al's (1998) behavioural model of information-seeking on the Web should be regarded as an information retrieval model. The model's name suggests it is a behavioural model. The model also has many elements similar to Aguillar's (1967) modes of environmental scanning. Choo combined and extended Aguilar's modes of environmental scanning and Ellis's information-seeking behaviour model into a new behavioural model of information-seeking on the Web. Choo identified four main modes of information-seeking on the Web: undirected viewing, conditioned viewing, informal search, and formal search. Being a hybrid model based on Ellis (1989) and Aguillar (1967), the Behaviour Model of Information-Seeking on the Web demonstrates the value of using multiple methods to collect data and has the potential to be extended or mapped to other information-seeking activities such as an information search. As such the model now also provides a systematic method to examine the relationship between information needs, search strategies, and search tactics.

(m) Web Information Seeking Behaviour: The present era is the era of information and knowledge revolution. Many electronic resources are available in the library. The increase in information available on the web has also affected the information-seeking behaviour of the users. Due to the evolution of computers and internet facilities, different types of information sources at different locations are available in one place (Fidel et.al. 1999) (Das and Patra). Today when people look for information they often go directly to the World Wide Web. The users with no formal search training use graphical web browsers and search engines to find and retrieve full-text documents. There has been a revolutionary shift in the information search and access process. The users face many problems while seeking and evaluating web-based information (Jenkins et.al. 2003). Web information seeking is an active stream of research that involves studying the searching of the public at large. These studies use transaction log data to analyze large numbers of queries by users of web search engines most notably studies of the Excite search engine (Jansen et. al. 2000, Spink, et. al. 2001). Comparing the results of three such studies, Jansen and Pooch (2001) determined that users pose an average of two queries per session, with the queries consisting on average of only two terms. Queries are simple with very little use of Boolean operators and relatively low use of other modifiers. The number of results typically viewed by users is ten or fewer per session. "Navigators and explorers Model" is also based on internet search methods of experienced information seekers (Navigators) and inexperienced information seekers (explorers). Navigators revisit domains and conduct sequential searches and have few deviations in searches whereas explorers visit many domains submitted many questions for seeking information. Robinson (2010) research suggested that in the process of seeking the information at work users rely on both people and information repositories. JISC study of Google Generations listed six characteristics of information-seeking behaviour as discussed earlier. Choo et. al. (1998) suggested conceptual models of ISB on the web, which refers to the activities related to assessing, searching, and dealing with information sources, especially in a networked environment. He also created a two dimensional model of ISB on which he combined the elements of Ellis ISB model and Aguliars four modes of organization scanning. Few models of ISB covered undirected viewing, conditional viewing, information search, and formal search (new behavioural model for information seeking) undirected reviewing covers viewing a wide range of sources. Conditional viewing relates to the seeker and views information on a selected topic (browsing, differentiating, and monitoring). Information search relates to an active search of information (differentiating, extracting, and monitoring). Formal search is planned structured and deliberate. The searcher has to invest time and effort in searching for information. The search is called as formal as it follows a method. These models increased the focus on web searching and internet searching, online databases or offline databases searching, etc. these are new data collection and mining tools, techniques, methods adopted by users for getting information in e-forms.

The different models that seem to be the most relevant models for this study are summarized in the following table. The important outcome of the analysis of Wilson's 1981 model is the recognition that information use had received little attention and, within information science, that statement is still relatively true today. Nor has much attention been devoted to the phenomenon of the informal transfer of information between individuals. The identification of these areas as relatively lacking in research attention demonstrates one of the functions of these models. The limitation of this kind of model, however, is that it does little more than provide a map of the area and draw attention to gaps in the research: it does not provide any suggestion of causative factors in information behaviour and, consequently, it does not directly suggest hypotheses to be tested. Dervin's Sense-making approach focuses on the need for information experienced by users within the context of their situations. This shifts the focus from the information-seeking processes characterised by Ellis, Kuhlthau, and Choo to the user and the context of the user's situation. The model highlights the existing gap between an information related problem that constitutes an information need and the information source that could provide the solution to the problem.

2.14. FACTORS AFFECTING INFORMATION SEEKING BEHAVIOUR

Line (1969) defined the factors that affected the information requirement of users namely age, experience, background, qualifications, seniority, solitary, or teamwork, persistence, thoroughness, motivation, willingness to accept help from others, awareness of sources, media of communication and storage, etc. Thus, he clearly stated that ISB is influenced by the factors noted above. An individual adopts different ways to satisfy an information need, which depends on certain factors and certain points which have to be considered when an individual decides on a certain course of action and it includes:

- Access to the source.
- Money matters the most which have to be considered
- The time involved is also an important factor
- The source whether it offers the answer to their problem
- Whether they will understand what the source provided as an answer

There are other factors also affecting the ISB viz. social, system, political, geographical, educational, etc. Social factors: a desire for information on such topics like information on fashion, music which may be openly available and looked upon in certain societies while in some societies it may be looked at behind closed doors.

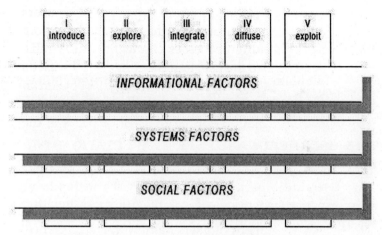

Fig. 2.12. Understanding the information seeking.

Political factors: The dictatorship political system may define the information on defence, freedom of speech, and expression as forbidden to a particular group while no availability of such information may motivate a person to resort to underground means.

Geographical factors: The geographical location of an individual also determines the means adopted by a person for searching for information.

Educational factors: Educated and uneducated may seek information differently.

A major emphasis on the study of information needs of social scientists occurred in England in the late 1960s. The investigation into information requirements of social scientists (INFORMS) was sponsored by the Office of Scientific and Technological Information (OSTI). The purpose of the study was to identify shortcomings in the traditional system of information acquisition to design improved information systems. The major conclusions of the study were:

- Social scientists placed a high amount of importance on finding references.
- Most of the formal information came from journals.
- They depended on informal channels such as consulting colleagues and experts for much of their information while library catalogues and librarians were of little use. Users have to consult the librarian to seek the desired information from various sources.

2.15. USER NEEDS AND USER'S EXPECTATIONS FROM LIBRARY

Users are important factors for libraries, without which an information system loses its complete purpose. In a library set-up, it is very important to understand who the users are, what their needs are, and how those needs can be satisfied using the library. If people are not using the library resources, it means that they are not been taken care of or they are not aware of the availability of information in the library. In some cases, the user has been a much-neglected element in the whole information business, but in the earlier and recent times emphasis on user, need has been laid by conducting various use and user studies. The user is termed as a user, consumer, patron, client, etc. but they are synonymic used in the library profession.

Line (1998) has defined expectations of users from the library and a few of them are summarised below

- An attractive building with suitable light and facilities required by users
- Long opening hours of libraries
- A variety of area for study purpose (individual space as well as space for group study)
- A coffee shop where one can relax, refresh, mix with other users and library staff
- Easy and good access to information in the library,

- Simple and speedy procedures for circulation
- The ability to access a variety of media from one workstation
- An easy to use easily accessible catalogue
- Speedy access to the resources not held in the library
- A shelf arrangement that aids borrowing
- Friendly behaviour of staff with users

The expectations of users defined by Line (1998) are true in the case of traditional libraries as well as technology-based libraries. But apart from these expectations, a few more could be added to the list after analyzing the trends as under:

- The collection in the library must be developed based on user needs and according to the mission and vision of the institute.
- More information services based on print and e-resources
- Guidance from library staff to search for proper information sources
- Increased usage of e-resources need orientation of information literacy for both users and library staff

2.16. INFORMATION SEARCHING VS. INFORMATION SEEKING

Information seeking relates to how people interact with information, how and when they seek information and what uses they make out of it. Seeking information from paper and online resources, many problems have been encountered and skills are needed to succeed in the specific acts associated with locating information either in a paper or online resource. Bates' articles on information searching tactics and search techniques (Bates 1979) promoted greater attention to the complexities of identifying sources and working one's way through resources to locate the desired information. A long line of research addressed that both search success and desirable design features in information systems to promote ease of use (Cochrane et al, (1983), Fidel, (1984), Hsieh-Yee (1993), Marchionni (1995), Spink (2001). Browsing is normally seen as the most unstructured method of information searching as described by Bates (2007), O'Connor (1993) and Rice (2001). In brief, information searching means hunting for information and browsing relates to unstructured information searching whereas information seeking is the process involving many activities together for getting and systematically using information.

2.17. ISB VERSES. GRATIFICATION THEORY

The gratification theory on ISB developed by Chatman (1991; p.42) identifies the underlying methods by which researchers can explore a minimally understood area in information studies. The theory has attempted to define problematic situations for poor people and new conceptual factors that influence their choice of a strategy. It has attempted to address a central issue of information use among poor people, even though they do not appear to be active seekers of information. This theory illustrates immediate gratification behaviour that appears prevalent in the lower working class. The findings suggest that no information-seeking will occur if respondents are convinced that a good future is more attributed to luck, rather than to one's investment of time or energy. In his attempt to determine the information-seeking strategies of engineers and scientists, Wolek (1972) made a study which is designed to assess their behaviour patterns when they needed to enrich their understanding of a technical subject before an interpersonal communication (Christie; 1981; p.159). The study has identified three basic and (3) Profesional peripheration. These factors are responsible for such methods to be adopted. Firstly, a user would tend to piggyback - giving information search a low priority; if there were higher priority demands on his or her time. Secondly, a person would be guided by previous experiences, especially concerning selecting appropriate sources of information. And finally, professional peripherin tended to be used when an understanding of the context of question/problem was felt necessary (ibid; p. 160). Holland's (1972; p. 160) study hypothesized that special communicators would be regarded by their colleagues as having especially high value as information sources and in term would have exposure to both a greater number and a greater diversity of information sources. In his result, he has suggested that the relationship between these two variables is usually very complex. Particularly, many variables like location, status, experience, telephone and travel budgets normally affect both information potential and information exposure.

2.18. ECONOMICAL WAYS FOR COLLECTION DEVELOPMENT

Users need pinpointed information within no time from different sources There is a need to design a system in libraries for developing proper collection and services to be provided to users based on their needs. It is not possible to satisfy all the users but the facilities provided can be easily made available and can be used by everyone according to their preferences. In addition to this user-centric services can also be introduced using online searching of e-resources. To re-engineer the practices in libraries librarians have to observe and understand the user needs. The library can also construct a profile of its user's interest and match it regularly against the available databases. Librarians need to listen and learn to find out the requirements of the clientele and make provision of information sources accordingly. This can be successfully achieved only if libraries measure their performances and undertake ISB studies and user studies

2.19. USER EDUCATION: CONCEPT AND MEANING

It is an acknowledged fact that the various types of users from teachers to students, scientists to engineers, managers to workers, business people to housewives, and so on, do not make optimum use of library and information resources. The reasons are no far to seek. The growth in the size of information sources in a variety of subjects has been making it difficult for users to find the needed documents. Coupled with this is the impact of information communication technology in recent years which has led to change in the format of documents making it further difficult to access the required sources. This makes it imperative for users to learn the ways and methods for easy access to valuable sources of information. The librarian and his staff may take some steps to impart some basic training to the users in the use of information services and sources.

In library and information science literature, many terms such as 'initiation', 'bibliographic instruction', 'user education', 'user orientation', and 'user assistance' have often been used interchangeably. However, the activities included in these categories are interrelated and influence each other. 'orientation' programme aims to familiarize the users with a particular library and information system and to help them through their problem. On the other hand, 'user education' generally consists not only of the orientation of the user in the practices and methods prevailing in a particular library system but also of the knowledge regarding the structure of subject literature, its development, its information resources, etc. In the words of Mews, "user education is the instruction given to readers to help them make the best use of a library." According to Tocatlian, user education may be defined to include any effort or programme which will guide and instruct existing and potential users. Wilson defined user education as the process whereby potential users of information are made aware of the value of information in specialized fields of activities. So, the traditional user education programmes are designed to make the users aware of what resources exist in the library, promoting them, and how best these can be used by individual users to find suitable information. It is clear from the above that user education is instructing and guiding the users on how to use the library. A user education programme, therefore, helps them to learn library and information practices, methods, services, and sources on their own.

2.19.1. Objectives of User education

Academic libraries support the teaching and research needs of institutions they serve. It is the libraries' responsibility to ensure that the use of its information sources, resources, and services are maximized to benefit its users, hence the necessity for user education programmes. Developments in computers, microelectronics, and communication technologies have radically changed the library and information environment. Gone are the days of stand-alone libraries, in which a library was judged less by the quality of its resources and services than by the number of documents it had available. Traditional libraries were dominated by print publications and the access mechanisms were also by and large manual. The paradigm shifts from stand-alone libraries to library and information networks, available via the Internet, can provide end-users with a seamless connection to Internet-based services. Moreover, we are surrounded by automated, digital, and virtual libraries as well as by networked data, specialized networks, and library networks. Multimedia and the Internet have further made the job of library and information professionals more challenging. Some of the basic objectives of user education and training are as follows:

- To create an awareness and understanding of the basic relevant library and information sources and services,
- To bridge the gap between the potential user and the library collection,
- To enhance users' abilities to select appropriate information sources and systems for a given information need,

- To offer instruction in the effective and efficient use of the available library facilities and resources,
- To develop users' knowledge and skills to access or retrieve the information required, and
- To help in the assessment of the existing library and information resources and services.

Thus, the long term objective is to make the user-library and information system interface more productive and to improve the use of resources and services.

2.19.2. User Education: Need

The following factors may explain the need for user education programmes:

(a) Growth of Information : In recent years, as a result of activities of various institutions, research and development organizations, individuals, etc. there has been an increase in information to the extent that it has become almost difficult to keep track of it. This growth is further compounded by the growth in the interdisciplinary and multidisciplinary subjects. Also, many information sources are being brought out in digital form such as CD-ROMs, DVDs, etc. while many others are available online. For efficient and effective use of these sources, and to retrieve the required information out of a mass of information, user education and training have become necessary.

(b) Non-use of Library Resources : The library is a service institution, adds new documents to its stock now and then for its users. But user studies about the use of library resources have reported that many of the documents in different subjects remain unused for various reasons. It is a great challenge for librarians. User education will help to encourage the better use of available resources.

(c) Unfamiliarity with Library System : Most of the library users are not well familiar with the way the documents are organized; they are not well familiar with the search process from the online public access catalogue, online databases, computer-based retrieval system, and so on. The user education programme will motivate them to have easy and efficient access to information stored in various sources. These are only some of the important reasons for initiating user education programmes in the library and information systems. Other reasons may include new methods of information transfer, changes in the physical format of documents, lack of proper guidance in the library, and so on.

2.20. METHODS OF USER EDUCATION

As no single method of user education is a panacea for all categories of users, many methods are available for this purpose. Nancy Fjallbrant and Ian Malley have identified the following three groups of methods:

1. Group Instruction : For providing instructions to users in groups they included:

(a)   Lecture method
(b)   Seminar/Tutorial/Demonstration method
(c)   Guided tour

2. Individual Instruction : Teaching methods generally used for individual instruction are:

(a)   Practical exercise
(b)   Self-instructional material (tours, signs, etc.)
(c)   Individual help

3. Group and Individual Instruction : For providing instructions both to groups and individual, the following methods are included:

(a)   Films
(b)   Videotape
(c)   Tape/slide
(d)   Audiotape

(e) Printed media (books, printed guides, etc.)

It may, however, be mentioned that the choice of teaching methods depends upon the learning/teaching situation, the users, and the subject material available for the purpose. Some of the important methods are briefly discussed here.

(a) **Lecture Method:** This is the most common and popular method of teaching, particularly when a large group of students is involved. Delivering lectures about the use of the library and its resources, and how best to use them is a technique used by the librarian/reference librarian. Lectures, supported by the PowerPoint (ppt) technique, can become quite effective in communicating the information to the audience.

(b) **Seminars/Tutorials/Demonstrations :** Seminars, tutorials, and demonstrations are organized for small groups of users by the library. These are regarded as effective methods for awareness and imparting awareness about library sources and services. These methods come up with an opportunity for more useful interaction between the users and the library staff. The staff, by way of demonstration, can easily explain to the users how to use various references and information sources for retrieving needed information. The users may be given topic/s to search for information by consulting various references and other sources.

(c) **Guided Tour:** The basic objective of a guided library tour is to familiarize the users in a small group with the location of different sections of the library. These tours are generally conducted under the guidance of a senior library staff member and users are taken around the library building. This method is useful as the users get to know about the actual use of the catalogue, classification system being followed, photocopying section, circulation section, how to enrol members of the library and get books issued, and other library rules. In many libraries, self-guided tours with the help of printed booklets have also been followed. However, this method requires a lot of library staff time.

(d) **Audio-Visual Method :** This is yet another method of providing instructions to a group of users about library sources and services. The use of tape/slide medium or audiotapes in combination with printed material was considered suitable for user education in the 1980s and 1990s. It was possible to display with the help of audio-visual aids, how to make use of library resources, how the classification system works, how the circulation section performs the job, how to search information from reference sources, and so on. This method had the advantage of having a profound impact on the minds of the users. With the introduction of computers in libraries, this method is now replaced with the use of multimedia, and the like.

(e) **Video-Tapes :** Many libraries prepare short motion films for user education purposes on different aspects of library sources and services. The users can be explained about, say, how to use catalogue and find books, how to use various reference sources, the services offered by the library to its users and how to use them effectively, and so on. This method is useful when users are in a group. A well-prepared videotape or film can be useful to motivate users for making better use of the library and its resources. The only disadvantage is that the users have to view and listen to the entire programme and then seek clarifications if any.

(f) **Programmed Instruction :** Programmed instruction is a course of instruction given by library staff making use of a variety of media. The subject matter of instruction is generally divided into a logical sequence of short items. It is carried out utilizing printed books, automatic projection of slides, or computer-aided instruction programme. The advantage of programmed instruction is that the users while working at their own pace can actively participate in the learning process. They can also check the suitability of their responses immediately.

(g) **Computer Assisted Instructions:** It is regarded as a very useful means of programmed instructions for teaching the use of more complex bibliographic tools, use of catalogue, indexes, etc. The instructions are given to the users through a computer with inbuilt software. The instructions are presented in small steps, and there is no need for a human instructor. The user learner makes a response in a two-way conversation which determines the next step. It also provides immediate feedback to the users.

(h) **Signs and Informational Graphics :** One of the basic methods of user education is the use of sign systems and informational graphics. This method has been in use for since long, as the libraries have been using different types of signs. The sign system can be grouped into two main types, viz. signs related to direction finding, and signs related to the use of library resources. It is observed that to make the signs most effective for user orientation they must be carefully planned concerning position, content, and presentation.

(i) **Individual Instructions :** The reference desk is the vantage point for the reference librarian where he meets the user. Library instructions provided to the individual user when he approaches the reference desk for help is one of the best ways of user education. It is the easiest way to help the needy user by teaching him how to find out the required information. In this process, the user can learn about the use of the library and its resources.

(j) **Library Pathfinders :** Printed guides have been found very useful as a method of user education. An alternative to these guides has been developed as library pathfinders. A library pathfinder is "a kind of map to the resources of the library; it is an information locator for the library user whose search for recorded materials on a subject of interest is just beginning." According to Online Dictionary for Library and Information Science pathfinder is "designed to lead the user through the process of researching a specific topic, or any topic in a given field or discipline, usually in a systematic step-by-step way, making use of the best finding tools the library has to offer."

It is a step-by-step instruction tool that will help users to find the basic documents required to begin a search on a topic. It is designed to gather all of the most useful, relevant, reliable, and authoritative resources on a variety of academic work-related or general interest topics. Pathfinders were originally developed in printed format in large academic libraries, but with the emergence of the World Wide Web, they may now act as portals to information about resources in a variety of formats including books, encyclopedias, bibliographies, journals, databases, almanacks, websites, search engines, etc. Each pathfinder may include systematically the scope of the topic, standard works, guides and bibliographies, indexing and abstracting services, call number, subject headings, etc. for literature searching. Pathfinders, therefore, help users, particularly students, find paths to information. This is why Jeanne Galvin suggests that the users of assignment-specific pathfinders that are readable and that can be used by students from completing assignments are more useful than more general pathfinders. Therefore, a library, to meet the information needs of its users, ought to prepare its specific pathfinders to guide the users. It has been observed from the above discussion that no single teaching method is all-encompassing for user education purpose. The suitability of teaching methods and media depends upon the teaching-learning situation, the subject concerned, and the users and staff involved in the training process.

2.21. PLANNING OF USER EDUCATION

The establishment of the UNISIST programme within UNESCO as an Inter-Governmental programme to stimulate and guide voluntary Co-Operation in the flow of S&T information at the national, regional and international levels, and the launching of national information systems, such as NISSAN in India, has focused attention on the need for training the users in the effective use of information. The UNESCO General Information Programme (PGI) has been making organized efforts to promote user education and training programmers through organizing seminars, workshops, and developing tools, publications, and guidelines. The 'UNISIST Guide for Teachers' and the 'Guidelines for Developing and Implementing a National Plan for Training in information use are the two very useful publications. Several countries, particularly the USA and UK, have made organized efforts in promoting programme for educating and training information users, and extensive literature in the field is available to guide the formulation of such programmes in India. Libraries provide a support service to the institutions they serve. It is important to understand the goals of the institution served to enable librarians to come up with a mission statement that should reflect the library's commitment to helping the institution achieve its goals. Thorough planning is needed to ensure that all activities carried out are towards meeting the institutional goals. Commitment to educate users should be reflected in the mission statement of the library. This should be followed by a written user education policy. User education programmes should aim to make all users aware of the information resources available, both directly in the library and from external sources, and enable users to enjoy the search for information. It is interesting to note that many of the objectives listed by libraries in this study stressed the self-sufficiency of users through a successful user education programme. Written policies and objectives on user education provide a basis for self-evaluation. This could be used to answer questions like, is the user education programme achieving what it was set out to achieve? If not more detailed studies on user information needs should be conducted. User education programmes need continuous revision to keep up to date with the changing information environment. Written objectives for instruction should be derived from the written profiles of the information needs of the users. Universities have unique identities "each university library must design its course to meet the immediate needs of its clientele as well as fit into the university teaching programme". This is evident in the responses; some libraries' concern is introducing first-year students to the library "some of whom have never used a library before". Some specific components of user education are:

- Librarians introducing new students, some of who come from school systems where there are generally, no school librarians or well-established libraries, to the complexities of university library facilities.
- Librarians familiarizing users, who have little or no information-seeking skills at all with a broad range of library resources to develop library skills.
- Librarians educating users on how to find materials manually or electronically using on-line public access catalogues and CD-ROMs.

2.21. LIMITATIONS OF USER STUDIES

Librarians have conducted many user studies from time to time to assess the information needs of their user community. The results of these studies have provided the opportunity to know about the strengths and weaknesses of their collection and develop as per the users' needs. However, it has been observed that because of many complexities in the information needs these could not reflect a true picture. Some of the shortcomings occurring in the user studies may be as follows:

1. Objectives of the user study are sometimes not properly determined by the investigators, and they attempt to plunge into administering the questionnaire, etc.
2. Sampling techniques used by the investigators are not flawless. Selecting the right sample of users is a big problem in itself. The investigators are not able to give due consideration to the refined techniques of random sampling. Therefore, the resultant sample may be biased. This makes the results of the study lop-sided which do not reflect the true picture.
3. The size of the sample should be such as to reflect the entire population which, in most of the user studies, is not a representative one. This adversely affects the findings.
4. The composition of the user population is equally important, because the information needs of users working in an academic institution may be markedly different from those in government departments or industry, and so on.
5. Other variables such as age, education, experience, etc. also affect the information-seeking behaviour of users.
6. Statistical analysis methods chosen may not be appropriate for the type of data collected.

If these and other limitations are removed from the user studies in the future, the findings can be made more valid and reliable. The library and information systems can come out of their cocoon, shed their passive image, assume the proactive role, and promote their resources and services.

REVIEW QUESTIONS

1. Briefly elucidate the various types of information needed by the users'.
2. What do understanding about information-seeking behaviour?
3. Define the various factors influencing the information-seeking behaviour of users'
4. Classify the user studies
5. Elucidate the various models of information-seeking behaviour.
6. Explain the need for user education.
7. What are the methods in user education?
8. How do you plan the user education?
9. Narrate the limitations of user studies.

BIBLIOGRAPHY

1. Baxter, M. (Ed.) (1979a), "The analysis of qualitative data: a symposium", Sociological Review New Series, Vol. 27, pp. 648-827.
2. Baxter, M. (Ed.) (1979b), "Qualitative methodology", Administrative Science Quarterly, Vol. 24, pp. 520-671.
3. Belkin, N. (1978), "Information concepts for information science", Journal of Documentation, Vol. 34, pp. 55-85.
4. Douglas, J. (1976), Investigative Social Research, Sage Publications, Beverly Hills, CA. Eysenck, H.J., Arnold, W. and Meili, R. (Eds) (1972), Encyclopaedia of Psychology, Search Press, London.
5. Garfinkel, H. (1967), Studies in Ethnomethodology, Prentice-Hall, Englewood Cliffs, NJ.
6. Hollnagel, E. (1980), "Is information science an anomalous state of knowledge?", Journal of Information Science, Vol. 2, pp. 183-7.
7. Katz, D. and Kahn, R.L. (1978), The Social Psychology of Organizations, 2nd ed., Wiley, New York, NY, Ch. 13.
8. Line, M.B. (1974), "Draft definitions: information and library needs, wants, demands and uses", Aslib Proceedings, Vol. 26, p. 87. On user studies
9. Lucas, H.C. (1975), Why Information Systems Fail, Columbia University Press, New York, NY.
10. Menzel, H. (1960), Review of Studies in the Flow of Information Among Scientists, 2 Vols, Columbia University, Bureau of Applied Social Research, New York, NY.
11. Olson, E.E. (1977), "Organizational factors affecting information flow

in the industry", Aslib Proceedings, Vol. 29, pp. 124-9.
12. Paisley, W.J. (1965), The Flow of (Behavioral) Science Information – a Review of the Research Literature, Stanford University, Palo Alto, CA.
13. Payne, R. and Pugh, D.S. (1976), "Organizational structure and climate", in Dunnette, M.D. (Ed.),
14. Handbook of Industrial and Organizational Psychology, Rand McNally, Chicago, IL, pp. 1125-73.
15. Roberts, N. (1975), "Draft definitions; information and library needs, wants, demands and uses: a comment", Aslib Proceedings, No. 27, pp. 308-13.
16. Roberts, N. (1976), "Social considerations towards a definition of information science", Journal of Documentation, Vol. 32, pp. 249-57.
17. Royal Society (1948), Royal Society Scientific Information Conference, London, 1946, Royal Society, London, report and papers submitted.
18. Wersig, G. (1971), Information-Kommunikation-Dokumentation, Verlag Dokumentation, Pullach bei Munchen.
19. White, A.R. (1974), "Needs and wants", Philosophy of Education Society, Proceedings, Vol. 8, pp. 159-80.
20. Wilson, T.D. (1979), "Information uses in social services departments", in Henriksen, T. (Ed.), Proceedings of the 3rd International Research Forum in Information Science, Statens Bibliotekskole, Oslo.
21. Wilson, T.D., Stratified, D.R. and Mullings, C. (1979), "Information needs in local authority social services departments: a second report on Project INKS", Journal of Documentation, Vol. 35, pp. 120-36.

Unit 3

OBJECTIVES
- Growth and development of the concept of informetrics
- Understand the term librametrics, Biometrics and Scientometrics
- Evolution of Classic Informetric Laws
- Implications of Informetric Laws
- Understood New trends in Informetrics

INTRODUCTION

The twenty-first century has witnessed rapid development in the field of Library and Information Science. Various knowledge theories were developed to give a new look to the existing practices followed in information services prevailing in various information centres. New interpretations invalidating the existing theories were originated. One of the major fields so developed is Informatics. It is a kind of scientific information activity and, at the same time, a part of information science and studies various metric aspects of its study object to enhance the information activity as well as the efficiency of information establishments (Sengupta, 1991, p197-227). To make good use of the efficiency and adaptability of products of information establishment, all metric aspects of informatics have been taken care of in this system.

EVOLUTION OF THE CONCEPT OF INFOMETRICS

The term 'Infometrics' is generally used as a broad term comprising all metrics studies related to Information Science, including Bibliometric (bibliographies, libraries ...), Scientometrics (science policy, citation analysis, research evaluation ...), Webometrics (metrics of the web, the internet or other social networks such as citation or collaboration networks). Informetrics was introduced by Prof.Otto Nacke, Director, Institute of Informetric and Scientometrie, Bielefeld, West Germany in 1979. The term was adopted immediately by All Unions Institute for Scientific and Technical Information and through VINITI's persuasion; it soon got the agreement of the FID. It is a concept introduced and practised by FID (International Federation of Documentation) and it considers information as an important translatable commodity, a basic component for socio-economic development of a country.

Informetrics covers all aspects of quantitative analysis of information transfer, irrespective of the media. As a member of the FID committee, Sengupta, LN. has sent a detailed note on Informetry to Prof. Nacke, and a brief version of it states that: "informetrics is the well-practiced measuring technique of the Information Science. It is operative mostly through the techniques of statistical and mathematical calculus. Informetrics deals with all aspects of information. In the era of the literature explosion, Informetrics is considered as a vital commodity for the generation of human knowledge, and this commodity is a transactive one. In addition to information handling, the information storing and information transferring at National and International level, it integrates and consolidates various mathematical and statistical measuring techniques to highlight the importance of information, its productivity, information theories like utility, cybernetics, stochastics, games and also on decision making."

Informetric studies signify the new approach to the scientific study of information flow: the improved bibliometric methods are applied not only to scientometric studies and research evaluations of science and technology (S&T) but also to the analysis of their mutual, societal, industrial and other specific relations. While bibliometrics is traditionally associated with the quantitative measurement of documentary materials. Informetrics aims also to study other types of information materials, such as websites, internet links, voice, sounds, artworks etc. as explained by Worme. Methods from the social sciences and humanities, as well as experimental research in the natural sciences, are normally applied in various contexts, serving as a base for careful validation and ensuring the scientific value of the analysis.

The twentieth century may be described as the century of the development of metric sciences- Iibrametrics, bibliometrics, sdentornetrlcs, Technometrics, informetrics, biometrics, sociometries, econometrics and lastly cyber metrics or webometrics. Of these, cybernetics is the most recent and has been developing during the last few years.

STATISTICAL BIBLIOGRAPHY TO WEBOMETRICS

The origin of the concepts of Informetrics can be traced back to the first use of the term 'statistical bibliography' by E.W. Hulme in 1923 "to denote quantitative techniques as applied to libraries.:" Hulme's work, which is considered as second reported work on bibliometrics, using document counts to provide insight into the history of Science and Technology. Bibliometric methods have been applied in various forms for a century or more. Sengupta (1992)5 claims that Campbell (1896)6 produced the first bibliometric study, using statistical methods for studying subject scattering in publications.

Some of the early work includes that of Cole and Eales (1917), which is claimed to be the first bibliometric study (although using the old terminology of 'statistical bibliography'). They studied the growth of literature in comparative anatomy for the period 1550-1860. They mainly analyzed the fluctuations of interest and distribution of literature among countries.' The first recorded study of citation data (being the third bibliometric study) was carried out by Gross and Gross" in 1927. The coining of the term 'bibliometrics' is frequently credited to Pritchard (1969), who proposed the term 'bibliometrics' to replace the title used and somewhat ambiguous term of 'statistical bibliography'. Paul Otlet (1934) had previously employed the use of the French equivalent of the term 'bibliometric' in his book titled 'Treatise on documentation'", Pritchard defined the new bibliometrics widely.

The term 'librametry' was first proposed in 1948 by Ranganathan' for the design and development of library buildings and furniture, types and varieties of book sizes and shapes for the housing of books, and library service (at ASLIB conference held in Lemington Spa). He also illustrated a few examples of the application of statistics to Library Science in a paper presented at DRTC in 1969.

In 1969, Nalimov and Mulchenko13 coined the Russian equivalent of the term 'Scientometrics' (naukometriya). The term had gained wide recognition with the founding in 1977 of the journal 'Scientometrics' by Tibor Braun in Hungary. According to its subtitle, 'scientometrics includes all quantitative aspects of the science of science, communication in science, and science policy'. It originated from USSR and was practised in East European countries, especially in Hungary, for quantification of science at the individual, institutional, national and even international level. Technometrics, on the other hand, is recognized as a separate field. The scope of the journal 'Technometrics', founded in 1959 in the US in the development and use of statistical methods in Physical, Chemical and Engineering Sciences.

In 1984 an FID committee, with very broadly defined objectives in the provision of research and technical data, was constituted on Informetrics under Nacke's chairmanship, where 'Informetrics' was taken as a generic term for both bibliometrics and scientometrics. This usage was adopted in the VINm monograph by Gorkova with the Russian title Infometriya (Informetrlcs)". However, the term was not widely adopted until 1988 when Brookes15 at the First International Conference on Bibliometrics and Theoretical aspects of Information Retrieval held at Umburg University Centrum, Belgium. He suggested that an 'Informetrics' which subsumes Bibliometrics and Scientometrics, for both documentary and electronic information, may have a future and could be included in the name of the second international conference on the subject."

In the second conference held at University of Western Ontario, Canada in 1989, Brookes endorsed 'Informetrics' as a general term for Scientometrics and Bibliometrics, with Scientometrics taken as leading to policy studies and Bibliometrics conceded more to library studies." The status of the term 'Informetrics' was enhanced in the 3rd International

Conference on Informetrics held at DRTC, Bangalore in 1991. The fourth conference held in Berlin, Germany in 1993, all the three terms were used." At this conference, the International Society for Scientometrics and Informetrics (ISSI) was founded and the subsequent conferences have been held biennially under the society's auspices. The list of conferences is listed on the website of ISS.

CONCEPTS AND TERMS IN METRIC STUDIES

Authors differ in defining the three closely related metric terms Bibliometrics, Scientometrics, Informetrics and Webometrics. Bibliometrics developed mainly in the west and arose from statistical studies of bibliographies. The term Sclentometrks was used mainly in the East (Russia) and is defined as the study of the measurement of scientific and technological progress. The term Bibliometrics ties too narrowly to libraries and the documentary origin of the field and can restrict this term to the mathematical study of libraries and bibliographies. Scientometric, on the other hand, deals mainly with science policy applications. Brookes, who advocates the use of the term 'informetrics', a term which takes cognizance of the fact that modern technology has imposed on us new non-documentary forms of knowledge representation and its transmission and dissemination.

(a) Bibliometrics

In 1969, Pritchard coined the term bibliometrics and defined it as 'the application of mathematics and statistical methods to books and other media of communication...' Its purpose was: "to shed light on the processes of written communication and of the nature and course of development of a discipline (in so far as this is displayed through written communication through counting and analysing the various facets of written communication".

Broadus (1987) reviews various other definitions and then provides the following definition: " ... the quantitative study of physical published units, or bibliographic units, or of surrogates of either..., He observed that Pritchard not only originated the new use of the term but also began a long series of definitions for it, frequently wide-ranging and vague concerning the exact object of study.

(b) Scientometrics

Scientometric has typically been defined as the "quantitative study of science and technology", for example in the special topic issue of the Journal of the American Society for Information Science (JASIS) on S&T indicators, edited by Van Raan." Brookes gives further insight into the use and definition of Scientometrics: The term Scientometrics, nurtured by Tibor Braun, has become fruitful in science policy studies. The term has now established a significant role in the social sciences. Applications have so far been restricted to the exploitation of the citation data provided by LSI but further refinements are now being critically examined. Though the techniques of scientometrics and bibliometrics are closely similar their different roles are distinguished by their very different contexts.

(c) Informetrics

A brief definition is implicitly provided by Egghe and Rousseau (1990) in the subtitle of their book: "Informetrics: quantitative methods in library, documentation and information science." In their view, "Informetrics deals with the measurement, hence also the mathematical theory and modelling of all aspects of information." It is mathematical meta information, i.e., a theory of information on information, scientifically developed with the aid of mathematical books. Tague-Sutcliffe provides the following definition: "Informetrics is the study of the quantitative aspects of information in any form, not just records or bibliographies and in any social group, not just scientists. Thus it looks at the quantitative aspects of informal or spoken communication, as well as recorded, and of information needs and uses of the disadvantaged, not just the intellectual elite. It can incorporate, utilize, and extend the many studies of the measurement information that lie outside the boundaries of both bibliometrics and scientometrics... Two phenomena that have not, in the past, been seen as a part of bibliometrics or scientometrics, but fit comfortably within the scope of informetrics are definition and measurement.

USE OF INFORMETRICS

Informetrics bibliometric analysis may be classified under two broad groups. One describing the characteristics of literature (descriptive studies), and the other examining the relationship formed between components of literature (behavioural studies).

Tague-Sutcliffe describes the following uses of informetrics:

- Statistical aspects of language, word, and phrase frequencies, in both natural language text and indexes, in both printed and electronic media.
- Characteristics of authors - productivity measured by the number of papers or other means, degree of collaboration.
- Characteristics of publication sources, most notably the distribution of papers in the discipline over journals.
- Citation analysis: distribution over authors, papers, institutions, journals, countries; use in evaluation; co-citation based mapping of disciplines.
- Use of recorded information: Library circulation and in house book and journal use, database use;
- Obsolescence of the literature, as measured both by using' and citation;
- Growth of subject literature, database, libraries, concomitant growth of new concepts;

- Definition and measurement of information and
- Types and characteristics of retrieval performance measures.

APPLICATIONS OF BIBLIOMETRICS

The sub-disciplines of bibliometrics include statistics, operation research, bibliometrics distribution and bibliometrics laws, citation analysis, circulation theory, information theory and theoretical aspects of information retrieval. The bibliometrics study besides its theoretical content has various practical applications in library management and deciding science policy on researches. Some of these practical applications of bibliometrics listed by Mahapatra are as follows:

- The bibliometrics study aims to improve the bibliographical control because bibliometrics analysis helps to know the size and character of literature in different fields.
- A major area of bibliometrics study is to determine statistics of literature relating to the country of origin, subject, form and language distribution of documents as well as their incidence of translation.
- The bibliometric study derives the subject relationships which suggest desirable general patterns of secondary service coverage.
- The citation data analysis and the volume of publication in year wise can be used in planning retrospective bibliographies which will provide some indication of both the age of material used in a discipline and to the extent to which more recent publications supersede the older ones, if at all.
- The bibliometrics analysis helps in the comparative assessment of the secondary service, particularly when related to overall figures on the size of literature and to subject links.

- The bibliometrics data also helps in taking some management decisions.
- The citations data also determines the list of highly cited journals or books, which can be used in deciding while discarding the stock of the library.
- Citation analysis can find out subject relationships which help in suggesting titles of journals relevant to a given discipline in a particular library.
- The bibliometric study also provides information about the structure of knowledge and pattern of communication

In general, Sengupta summarized the applications for bibliometrics as:

- Quantify research and growth of different areas of knowledge.
- Estimate comprehensiveness of secondary periodicals.
- Identify uses authorship of documents on various subjects.
- Measure usefulness of ad hoc and retrospective SDI service.
- Experimental models correlating or bypassing the existing models.
- Identification of core journals in different disciplines to formulate a need-based acquisition policy within the limited budgetary provision without detriment of the research interest of the parent organisation;
- Initiate effective multilevel network system.
- Regulate inflow of information and communication
- Development norms for standardisation.

SUBFIELDS OF INFORMETRICS

Based on the kinds of data generally examined, different sub-fields of informetrics have emerged. A major subfield of informetrics is citation studies. It was the publication of the family of citation indexes and similar tools by LSI, Philadelphia that led to the emergence of informetrics as a major branch of Information Science. The other areas ' and their components are:

(a) Citation studies

Informetric data relate to:
- Citation measures; the citation frequency, impact factor etc.
- Co-citation and co-reference measures (bibliographic coupling etc.).
- The measure of ageing and obsolescence (citation data is used for measuring ageing and obsolescence of papers in periodicals; for monographs, this is measure by circulation data).

(b) Word-related Analysis

Informetric data related to:
- Word frequency measures; co-word analysis; co-classification data analysis, etc. (Cluster analysis and Correspondence analysis are among the techniques used).

(c) Author - Related Analysis

Informetric data related to:
- Frequency distribution of publications over authors and of authors over publications.
- Analysis of data relating to author affiliations/ institutions, countries/ region.
- Co-author matrices (Degree of collaboration, collaboration indexes etc.).

(d) Literature Growth studies

Informetrics data relate primarily to:

- Growth of literature in the discipline (or even a periodical) over some time: The effort is to map the growth and fit it into some mathematical model.

(e) Theoretical Informetrics

This is largely concerned with establishing and verifying informetric laws; the laws relating to a wide range of informetric data identified above.

(f) User studies

The ultimate measure of the quality of a library collection and its services is based on the extent and mode of its use. User studies are very much useful for wise planning of information systems. It is the thorough examination of the users of a library or information centre in terms of their types, the categories of documents and services they use, the urgency with which they need the documents and services, etc., using one or more of the approved methods."

A large number of techniques have been developed in the past few decades to find out the needs of library users. Most of them are concerned with different types of users and degrees to which user needs are satisfied, as listed by Ravi Chandra Rao.

1. To make a careful and intensive study of the library situation (in the late 1950s).
2. To measure the adequacy of a library collection for present and possible future library programmes (in the late 1950s).
3. To discover mathematical models for patterns of library use, concerning different types of users and also concerning different types of documents (in the late 1960s and early 1970s).

Various methods are employed to conduct user studies and the studies vary from one study to another. In many studies, questionnaires are used for collecting data. Periodical visits, checklists, library statistics, correspondence and interviews are also used in various combinations. Some of the other well-known methods are diary method, observation method, and library records analysis.

The major element of user studies in bibliometrics is to analyse the recorded results or products of the use of information tools, techniques. systems and resources. For example, statistical analysis of citations helps to determine the extent of use of different kinds of documents, the facts of a subject etc. of a specific field of study. The results obtained through user studies can be applied in the following activities:
- Collection development and managing
- Improvement in the services
- Introduction of new services
- Design of information systems and services

(g) Circulation studies

The circulation section is the most important unit of a library or information centre which mainly delivers the documents to the readers without any delay. An analysis of circulation data gives rise to information related to the volume of use by type of documents of different age, seasonal variations in transactions etc.

The circulation data can be used to measure the resources. These data can also be used to decide the acquisition and circulation policies of the library. For meaningful results, however, circulation data should be correlated with other variables such as data information on teaching methods adopted, course content and examination procedures of an academic institution. In addition to this, the circulation data may be correlated to data based on characteristics of users and documents, such as sex, status of users, subject of the document, field of interest of users etc. This will help in the collection development and its management programmes in a library.

(h) Document and content analysis

Content analysis is mainly used to analyse the records of human experience and knowledge, or "it is used to describe the content of communication 'messages' - that is materials such as novels, newspapers, reference tools or a variety of additional media and descriptive tasks relating to their contents". It is defined by Busha and Harter as a "procedure designed to facilitate objective analysis of the appearance of words, phrases, concepts, themes, characters, or even sentences or paragraphs contained in printed or audio-visual materials. The purpose of content analysis in social science research is to study the contents so that the conceptual analysis of thought contents of the document can be done. In the field of Library and Information Science, content analysis is used as a technique to analyse numerically the intellectual organization of information and services. The main area of Library and Information Science where the use of content analysis is applied may be grouped as

- use in information storage and retrieval
- application in user studies
- management

NEW TRENDS IN INFORMETRICS

Quantitative studies based on research publications became commonly known as 'bibliometric' studies'. Under this approach, a series of new methods and techniques were developed and used by scholars on a wider concept called 'Informetric analysis'. New concepts and terms like exponential growth of science, invisible college, gatekeepers etc. emerged and became popular over a wider scientific domain. Using the Informetric approach, knowledge representation at the level of scientific speciality, intellectual structures, informal and formal networks in both natural and social science could be investigated.

ANALYSIS OF FULL TEXT

One problem of bibliometrics is that, in mainly studying bibliographies, it has been limited to a small subset of document properties. Now, with full-text documents increasingly available in electronic format, informetrics can study collections of whole documents. Full document analysis is drawing computational linguistics closer to informetrics in the area of subject (content) analysis and the mapping of scientific fields. A shift to full document analysis, and more generally to the study of cyberspace, should promote the metric component of informetrics.

MEASUREMENT OF INFORMATION

Measurement of information can be done with the relevance of users' information need and the value of information service to the user community. Various attempts to measure knowledge succeeded only to suggest certain ratios of measures and models. They provide mainly a ratio, ie comparative growth of information in a particular area about a set of publications. An exemplar of the psychometrics approach is TagueSutcliffe's129 construction of a measure for the informativeness of documents to readers. The value of even a simple measure of subject aboutness in the compilation of literature collections for informetric analysis was demonstrated by Wilson130, who used a content-analysis approach, validated by Abstracting & Indexing services judgements.

Informetrics on the World Wide Web The development of informetrics will be shaped considerably by the continuing technological revolution, with its shift from paper to the electronic medium. In this new realm, Harter says that "traditional bibliometric research continues on electronic documents in electronic journals using enhanced analytical power, and better facilitated by digital libraries. In cyber metrics, web sites will play the same role as that of the documents in bibliometrics. The two important concepts that have emerged are situations (cited site) a cyber-counter part of citation and web impact factor. The citation concepts have been applied to hypertext systems, where hypertext links between documents can be thought of as a form of reference representing an acknowledgement of the linked document. The term 'citations' has been used by Rousseau to represent a hypertext linkage between web sites, to distinguish between citations received by published works and hypertext linkages between two documents. The concept of a Web Impact Factors has been proposed by Ingwersen (1998), where the websites and its pages correspond to journals and articles respectively. This impact factor is calculated as the number of link pages pointing to a given site/domain, divided by the number of pages on a given web site. Like the standard impact factor, the web impact factor serves as an indicator of web site's significance. While delivering Sarada Ranganathan Endowment Lecture at Institute of Information Studies, Bangalore in 1999, Egghe discussed Informetric aspects of the internet. In his presentation, he attempted to investigate the new world (virtual reality) of Internet and challenges that it offers for informetric research. Particularly, he discussed:

- The problems of data gathering
- The Internet version of the informetric laws
- Scientometric aspects of the Internet - can the clickable buttons (hyperlinks) in web pages replace the role of classical laws.
- References in journals/documents - Is there anything like web impact factor.

INFORMETRIC LAWS

According to Ravi Chandra Rao, "one of the features of informetric studies is the use of mathematical and statistical models to analyse fundamental problems, which arise while operating information systems. In such studies, explicit attention is given to the construction of modelling as a unifying activity with an avenue to future growth. One of the principal aims of science is to trace, amidst the tangled complex of the external factors, the operation of what are called laws to interpret a multiplicity of natural phenomena in terms of a few fundamental principles. help us in the development of theories to explain the pattern of occurrence of events.

(a) Classic Informetric Laws

Regularities in recorded discourse observed by early researchers in Informetrics are often referred to as 'laws'. The term 'law' is used by informaticians in its loosest sense, describing what in reality amounts to a mathematical generalization of an observed regularity in information production and use. A bibliometrics process may be described as a population of sources producing items at random in time. The classical informetric laws deal with:

1. Scattering and seepage of articles in different Periodicals-Bradford's law of scattering.
2. Productivity of authors in terms of scientific papers by them- Latka's law.
3. Pattern of the frequency of words in a text-Zipf's law.

Applications of these three distributions are more frequently reported on in Library and Information Science literature.

(b) Stochastic Model

The stochastic model, unlike the classical bibliometrics laws, treats bibliometrics processes as dynamic systems evolving. Consider, for example, the concept of core collection or nuclear zone of the most productive periodicals cited in the bibliography of a specific subject or the most used set of books in a subject. The Stochastic model seeks to stress the value of longitudinal empirical studies to show how bibliometrics data sets may evolve in time.

BRADFORD'S LAW

Samuel Clement Bradford (10 January 1878 – 13 November 1948) was a British mathematician, librarian and documentalist at the Science Museum in London. He developed Bradford's law" (or the regarding differences in demand for scientific journals. This work influences bibliometrics and citation analysis of scientific publications. Bradford founded the British Society for International Bibliography (BSIB) in 1927 and he was elected president of International Federation for Information and Documentation (FID) in 1945. Bradford was a strong proponent of the Universal Decimal Classification) UDC and of establishing abstracts of the scientific literature. Bradford's (1934) law states that; documents on a given "subject" is distributed (scattered) according to a certain mathematical function so that growth in papers on a subject requires a growth in the number of journals/information sources. The number of the groups of journals to produce a nearly equal number of articles is roughly in proportion to 1: n: n2 ..., where n is called the Bradford multiplier. For example, journals have as many papers on a given subject as a much larger number of journals, n, which again has as many papers on the subject as n^2 journals.

Bradford (1934) studied the title dispersion of useful papers in two areas: applied geophysics and lubrication by arranging the source titles in order of productivity and then dividing them into three approximately equal groups. Bradford concluded that the ratio of the titles in successive zones followed a common pattern, and proposed and following "law of scattering".

If scientific journals are arranged in order of decreasing productivity of articles on a given subject, they may be divided into a nucleus of periodicals more particularly devoted to the subject and several groups of zones containing the same number of articles as the nucleus where the number of periodicals in the nucleus and succeeding zones will be 1: a: a

In other words, only a small number of journals will be needed to supply the nucleus of paper on a given topic, assuming that the topic is a narrow scientific subject. Beyond the nucleus or first zone, however, the number of journals required to produce the number of papers increases dramatically. For example, if two journals are needed to supply the next 300 articles, sixteen journals will be needed to supply the next 300 articles.

IMPLICATIONS

The statistical regularity pointed out by Bradford's law provides an objective means of determining zones of relative richness or value to a given kind of library collection. This has implications for the acquisition process in a library. A library can safely stock the journals which belong to the core or nuclear zone. It is advisable to extend the purchase list to the next zones till the budget limits permit. If at all the budget is elastic, a point will be reached at which it would be desirable to obtain copies of articles in the journals on demand rather than subscribing to the journal. Lancaster provides an excellent hypothetical example of applying Bradford's law in periodical collection building while discussing the principle of diminishing returns Brookes (1969) is of the view that if the total expenditure on periodical provision is limited to the fraction 'f' of the sum needed to cover the subject completely, the buying of periodicals may be supplemented by the buying of photocopies of the relatively few relevant papers published in the peripheral periodicals.

We find the implications of the three kinds of scattering for the practical use of Bradford's law. If core journals (or other information sources) are selected from the frequencies of words or concepts, rather than subjects proper, then such cores may contain journals that are not relevant to users. The core may be "polluted" with journals not belonging to "the subject". Such journals may take the place of other journals "on the subject" that use different words or concepts. In other words, adequate indexing of documents is as relevant for providing Bradford distributions as for providing relevant documents to users. Besides, while the distribution of documents according to word frequencies is a rather mechanical, neutral, and "objective" process, the distribution of information sources according to the subject matter is a much more interpretative and political process. It is much more difficult to make operational implications of "subjects". What is a subject for one person need not be the same subject for another? The best way to generalize views about subjects is probably to consider different theoretical views or epistemologies regarding subjects. A pure mechanical view of selection must consequently be replaced by a reflective view in which the selector must justify the selection on value-based studies.

APPLICATIONS OF BRADFORD'S LAW

Several commentators have suggested solving practical journal collection management problems by using Bradford's law. The basic idea is to conduct Bradford analyses of journals - i.e., to sort out to the journals in Bradford zones – and thus to identify which belong to the core and which do not. Any Bradford analysis involves three steps:

1. Identify many or all items (usually articles) published in this field;
2. List the sources (usually journals) that publish the articles (or items) in rank order beginning with the source that produces most items;
3. While retaining the order of the sources, divide this list into groups (or zones) so that the number of items produced by each group of sources is about the same.

Nisonger (2008) argues in his textbook Management of Serials in Libraries that the following points are some of the "most obvious potentials" of Bradford analyses:

(a) Selection/deselection;
(b) Defining the core;
(c) Collection evaluation;
(d) The law of diminishing returns;
(e) Calculation of cost at various coverage; and
(f) Setting priorities among journals.

The current revolution in computer-aided, microanalytical techniques of information retrieval is largely justified by earlier studies of literature used in scientific research. These studies showed that a researcher's interest was widely scattered among formal titles and classifications and was much more extensive provided by exist than the coverage provided by existing bibliographic services. The important measures of scatter used in empirical studies are "title dispersion", which is defined as the degree to which the useful literature of a given subject area is scattered through several different books and journals.

Bradford did not conclude his study by simply stating his law verbally, but went to express it graphically by using experimental data, not noting himself that the graphical expression was not mathematically identical to the verbal formulation. He plotted R (n) (cumulative total of relevant papers) against log n (natural logarithms of a total of productive journals) and found that the data revealed an elongated s-shaped curve, the general form of which is shown in the figure. Part one of the curve, the initial concave portion, represents the higher density of the nuclear zone. Part two, the linear portion of the curve when data are plotted on a semi-log scale, is equivalent to Zipf (1949) distribution. Hence the commonly used expression the Bradford- Zipf distribution part three, often called the 'Groos drop', shows a departure from linearity for higher values of n, the reason for which is not yet fully understood (Groos, 1967). Brookes (1968), thought that the droop observed when there were omissions from the relevant literature.

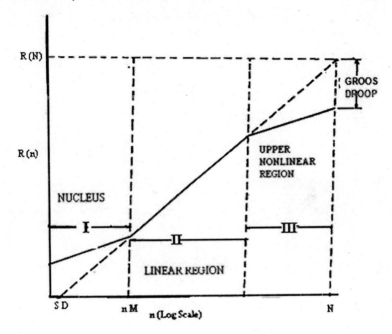

Fig. 3.1. Groos Droop
(*Source*: Sangam, 1985)

In the years following the publication of Bradford's Law papers by eminent researchers such as Vickery (1948), Brookes (1968) and Leimkuhler (1967) contributed to a partial understanding of the Bradford distribution partially because these contributors did not interpret the law in mathematically identical terms. Vickery extended the verbal formulation to show that it could be applied to any number of zones of equal yield, not only to the three zones that Bradford had used for his date (Vickery, 1948). Later Leimkuhler expressed the verbal formulation mathematically as is shown in the equation (Leimkuhler, 1967).

R (n) = j log (n/t+1) (n>n_m)

Where, R (n) = cumulative total of relevant papers found in the first n journals when all periodicals are ranked 1, 2, 3...n in order of decreasing productivity:

n = Cumulative number of journals producing

R (n) = relevant papers;

j and t = Constants defined in terms of others variables; and

n_m = the value of n beyond which the curve becomes linear.

Brookes in a study expressed the formula for the graphical version of Bradford's law beyond the nuclear zone and for N log as is shown in equation 2 (Brookes, 1968).

R (n) = N log (n/s) (n>n_m)

Where

N= total number of journals estimated to contain articles relevant to the subject of the search.

S= a constant calculated using experimental data.

Vickery (1948) in his paper noted that the verbal and graphical formulations were not mathematically identical. Once the disparity between the two formulations was recognized, the question arises concerning which of the two was more practical to apply to empirical data. Wilkinson (1972) devised a comparative test between the two formulations utilizing the same bibliographic data for four different subjects (agricultural, economics, muscle fibre, schistosomiasis, and mast cells. The test did not require the calculation of the nucleus (region 1 in figure 1). Instead, it utilized simple formulas for calculating N (the estimated total number of Journals containing articles relevant to the subject of the search) and R (N) (the estimated total number of papers produced by N). Only 'P' (number of journals) and 's' (the corresponding cumulative number of papers) had to be known to apply the formulas. Both P and S were obtained from a plot of the empirical data on semi-log paper. Although the value of P could be chosen anywhere in the linear portion of the curve, the point at which the initial concave portion of the curve turned into the linear region ($n=n_m$) was arbitrarily chosen to be equal to P and was used in determining the corresponding value of S. By identifying the plot 2S papers, the corresponding number of journals required to supply 2S, called q, was ascertained. The values obtained for S, P, and q, were then used for calculating N and R (N) for both the verbal and graphical expressions of Bradford's law. Wilkinson's (1972) test revealed that the data she considered the graphical rather than the verbal formulation was more consistent with the practical situation.

Verbal Formulation

$$N = \frac{S}{\log a} - \frac{P}{a-1}$$

Where, $a = \frac{q-p}{p}$

$$R(N) = \frac{a}{\log a} \log \left[\frac{s}{\log a} - \frac{(a-1)}{p} \right]$$

Graphical Formulation

$$N = \frac{S}{\log \beta}$$

Where $\beta = \frac{q}{p}$

$$R(N) = \frac{S}{\log \beta} \cdot \log \left[\frac{a}{\log \beta} \frac{\beta}{p} \right]$$

LOTKA'S LAW

Lotka, a bio mathematician, investigated the literature output of a sample of chemists and found that "... the number (of authors) making n contributions is about 1/n2 of those making one; and the proportion of all contributors, that make a single contribution, is about 60 per cent

$$P(n) = k/n^2$$

Where p is the number of authors producing n papers, and where k is a constant characteristic of a particular subject area.

Lotka gave an acceptably modern, mathematical description of his regularity that remains today as the (classic) Latka's law. However, Lotka's article was not cited until 1941 and his distribution was not termed 'Lotka's Law' until 1949, as said by Potter.

Book stein points out that the following theoretical model

$$F(x) = k/x^2 \quad x = 1, 2, 3 .... \quad K > O, \infty > O$$

Is a generalized version of Lotka's law; k and a are constants. In other words, the number of authors with x papers is proportional to $1/X^2$.

Price, also interested in scientists' productivity has defined a law developed from Lotka's stating that 'half of the scientific papers are contributed by the square root of the total number of scientific authors'. In other words, the Price's Square Root Law of Scientific Productivity states that $N^{1/2}$ sources yield a fraction 1/2 of the items

In most of these studies, the number of publications is considered as a measure of scientific productivity. There are four methods of counting of several publications.

Total counting/ normal (standard) counting : Each occurrence of an author is recognized and receives equal treatment, regardless of the number of authors associated with a given article. Therefore, an author receives equal credit, whether he or she is the only author of a publication or one of many. (each of the N authors receives a credit of 1)

Straight counting/first author counting: Only the first author is counted, based on the assumption that the first author is the primary contributor to a publication. In deriving Inverse Square Law of scientific productivity, Lotka adopted this method. (only the first of the N authors receives a credit 1)

Adjusted counting/ Fractional counting : Authors receive fractional credit or publications with multiple authors (each of the N authors receives a score of N/1)

Proportional counting : If an author has a rank R in a paper with N authors (R = 1, 2, 3 ... N), then he/she receives a score of $\frac{2}{N}\left[1 - \frac{R}{N+1}\right]$. In case of proportional counting this formula is obtained by dividing the absolute weights N + 1 – R by the sum of all ranks: $1 + 2 + ... + N = \frac{N(N+1)}{2}$.

There are two approaches generally used for organizing scientific productivity data i. Size-frequency: a standard frequency approach which models frequency of source f (x) as a function of the number of items x. It allows one to use traditional statistical techniques. ii. Rank-frequency: an approach which models the number of items g(x) as a function of the rank of the source r. Its emphasis on those sources which have the most productive items, then those having small ranks

$$r = 1, 2, 3, 4 ...$$

Lotka's suggestion led to a whole extent of studies on scientific productivity. This productivity studies have gained momentum in the post-second world war period. It has culminated in the rise of a new discipline called scientometrics. Scientometrics is defined as the study of the measurement of scientific and technological progress. It provides an understanding of the structure of scientific activity, the disciplines being researched, the organizations involved, the strength and weakness in the scientific groups and their communication channels at different levels of aggregation. It pursues with the direction of econometrics in the use of quantitative data, concepts and models and extensive use of mathematical and statistical techniques of modelling and data analysis. Scientific productivity has been studied from different angles. Impact of social change on scientific productivity and some of the approaches are made like the relationship of publication output on scientific recognition, identification of elites in different disciplines, the occurrence of discoveries in different cultures etc. Price, who had discovered that development of science since Babylon and planned the growth of big science from little science had observed that Lotka s law applied equally well to the productivity of scientists in the 17th as well as in the 20th century. This meant that majority of publications initiated from a few of the people. It is already seen as Prices Square Root Law (SRL). In this way, the conclusion of an extensive review of early studies of scientific productivity made by Narin was scientific talent. It was highly concentrated in a limited number of individuals.

ZIPF'S LAW

It is perhaps the most widely quoted and applied empirical regularity in the recorded discourse, having applications in Social Science disciplines, such as Linguistics. George Kingsley Zipf', a philologist with a wide interest in J-shaped distributions, developed an observation made earlier by Estoup and others on word occurrences. Zipf's law states that if words are ranked according to their frequency of occurrence (f), the nth ranking word will appear approximately k in times where k is a constant or $f(n) = k/n$.

Zipf's law proved to be unacceptably inaccurate too often, and the regularity is now more typically described by a better equation derived by Mandelbrot, known as Mandelbrot Law. It states that

$$(r + m)^B f = C$$

where r is the rank of word f is the frequency and B and C are constants dependent on the corpus.

Zipf's equations have traditionally used a rank-frequency approach; however, size-frequency forms have also been used by many informetricians. The three basic and most popular laws in informetrics are discussed above. Bradford's Law explains the scattering of articles on specific subjects in various journals while Lotka's Law centres on author productivity and Zipf's Law deals with distributions of occurrence of words. Each of these laws is based on empirical studies and they are similar to each other and they can be represented as a special case of a hyperbolic distribution. Several such power-law relations are found to occur in bibliographic studies of scientific journals, articles, authors and citations.

The discoveries of empirical laws of informetrics have led to a series of studies that can be broadly differentiated into two-quantitative and qualitative. The early statistical studies of Cole and Eales, Hulme, Lotka, Zipf and Bradford belong to the quantitative category. On the other hand, qualitative application studies emphasize the practical utilization of research findings.

INFORMETRIC MODELS

The trend in informetrics is mostly towards the discovery of theory and or generalized mathematical models. To provide a sound conceptual understanding of the empirical laws, many informetric models have been developed.

Ravi Chandra Rao, and Burrell, have argued that the negative binomial model explains the distribution of document circulation. A notable recent trend in informetrics is a renewed interest in time as a variable in the form of the informetric regularities. In a series of papers, Burrel has argued that time is not only essential for the appropriate modelling of the situations but also allows genuine practical applications of bibliometrics techniques which are not possible using the classical laws.us.

The most impressive of the stochastic compound distributions used in the study of the informetric regularities in the Generalized Inverse Gaussian Poisson (GIGP) distribution of Sichel. In his paper Simon, derived a mathematical solution for his basic model which he termed the Yule distribution, and which in the limit has the required Lotka form of the Inverse Power Law1.

Other Empirical models include:

Sengupta's law of Bibliometrics

In his bibliometrics law, Sengupta remarks that during phases of rapid and vigorous growth of knowledge in a scientific discipline, articles of interest to that discipline appear in increasing number in periodicals distant from that field. Mathematically Sengupta's law stands in the following form:

$F(X+Y) = a + b \log(x+.0)$, where $f(x+.0)$ is the enumerative number of references as contained in the first $(x+.0)$ most productive journals, x indicates the number of journals in the same discipline and y stands for the number of journals of unrelated disciplines $(Y > X)$, a and b are constants.

Garfield law of Concentration

Garfield talked about the number of journals involved in publishing the literature of a single field. He argues that a "basic concentration of periodicals is the common core or nucleus of all fields. In other words, the tail of the literature of one discipline consists, in large part, of the cores of the literature of other disciplines. So large is the overlap among disciplines that the core literature of all scientific disciplines involves a group of not more than 1000 journals.

Goffman's Epidemic Theory

Goffman and Newin use the epidemic theory to model

literature dynamics, especially in terms of growth and scattering of literature. This model is based on the rate of change over time in the expected number of susceptibilities, infective and removals. The theory shows that the process of diffusion of information (e.g. innovations) is analogous to the process of spread of epidemics and therefore, the diffusion process can be represented by the following set of differential equations.

$$\frac{ds}{dt} = .\beta sI - \gamma + U$$

$$\frac{ds}{dt} = .\beta sI - \gamma + 8$$

$$\frac{ds}{dt} = .\beta sI + y^i$$

Where 5, I and "R" are continuous functions of the real variables t; p is the rate of infection (acceptance) and $8r$ is the rate at which susceptible and removal and $Jl6$ is the rate at which a new supply of susceptible enters the population.

PRICE SQUARE ROOT LAW OF SCIENTIFIC PRODUCTIVITY

DeSella Price states that "half of the scientific papers are contributed by the square root of the total number of scientific authors." He predicts that the number of the elite in science is small compared to the total number of scientists. In his square root law, he claims that any population of size N contains effective elite of size.

Characteristics of Informetric distributions

Success-Breeds-Success Phenomenon

Price (1976), Simon (1955) and many others argue that the success breeds- success phenomenon characterizes bibliometrics distributions as they do in another social process.

De Solla Price's examples of the occurrence of the phenomenon in bibliometrics include the following:

(i) A journal that has been frequently used is more likely to be used again than an infrequently used journal;

(ii) An article in a journal, which has been cited many a time is more likely to be cited again than the one, which has been rarely cited;

(iii) An author of many papers is more likely to publish again than the less prolific one.

Similarly, Ravi Chandra Rao (1981) in his thesis argues that:

(i) Those documents, which have been borrowed frequently, are more likely to be borrowed again than those borrowed infrequently in an academic library in an academic year:

(ii) Those users who borrow documents frequently are more likely to borrow documents again than those who seldom borrowed documents in an academic year.

In statistics, such a phenomenon is generally described by a hyperbolic distribution function. Price also points out that the success-breeds-success phenomenon can be described by a negative binomial distribution, it is known as Yule distribution. Egghe (1999) in one of his lectures presented several generalizations of the phenomenon, particularly to discuss the production process that occurs in informetrics. His work extends the SBS principles of Simon and De Solla Price.

Bookstein (1976) briefly discuss the different bibliometric distributions that allow one to understand them as being different versions of a single theoretical distribution. He suggests the following to describe the bibliometric process:

$$I(x) = K/x^a = 1, 2, 3, ... k, œ > O$$

This function can be used to describe Zipf's, Lotka's and Bradford's laws as follows:

1. $f(x)$, the number of words occurring x times, is proportional to $1/x^z$
2. $f(x)$, the number of authors who have published x papers, is proportional to $1/x^z$
3. $f(x)$, the number of journals which contain x articles in a given subject, is proportional to $1/x^z$

This is also the view of Mandelbrot (1952)126. He suggested the following formula.

$$f(x) = \frac{k}{c\pi} \alpha xJ$$

$f(x)$ is the number words with rank x; k is a normalizing factor; "α" and "π" are constants.

Ravichandran Rao argues that the bibliometric distributions have the following characteristics in common.
1. Distributions are reverse J shaped;
2. Distributions are highly skewed;
3. Generally, the distributions have long tails;
4. The most general form of the distribution is $f(x) = c(x + a)^k c$, a and k are constants.
5. The bibliometric distributions are usually due to a success-breeds success phenomenon; it can be described by a negative binomial distribution.

The 80-20 Rule

The success-breeds-success phenomenon may be explained by the 8020 rule. The 80-20 rule states that 80 per cent of the items (number of citations received, articles number of publications etc) are accounted for by about 20 per cent of the sources (journals, authors etc.).128 Some of the other important informetric models are:
1. Logarithmic model of Brookes
2. Cumulative Advantage Distribution Model by Price

3. Mandelbrot's model structure of language expending and restating Zipf's law
4. Fairthorne's model linking Lotka's law and other laws
5. Vickery's model extending Bradfords distribution
6. Graphical model of Leimkuhler
7. Hills model of the negative binomial distribution
8. Naranan's Power law

Further investigation of these models is needed, but ultimately acceptance will depend on how satisfactorily they explain the regularities. There are many such models, distributions and measures in informetrics. These models, distributions and measures have an important role to play in the design and development of information systems. It is in this context that informetrics is considered as an important area of research in the field of Library and Information Science.

New trends in Informetrics

Quantitative studies based on research publications became commonly known as 'bibliometric' studies'. Under this approach, a series of new methods and techniques were developed and used by scholars on a wider concept called 'Informetric analysis'. New concepts and terms like exponential growth of science, invisible college, gatekeepers etc emerged and became popular over a wider scientific domain. Using the Informetric approach, knowledge representation at the level of scientific speciality, intellectual structures, informal and formal networks in both natural and social science could be investigated.

1. Analysis of full text: One problem of bibliometrics is that, in mainly studying bibliographies, it has been limited to a small subset of document properties. Now, with full-text documents increasingly available in electronic format, informetrics can study collections of whole documents. Full document analysis is drawing computational linguistics closer to informetrics in the area of subject (content) analysis and the mapping of scientific fields. A shift to full document analysis, and more generally to the study of cyberspace, should promote the metric component of informetrics.

2. Measurement of information : Measurement of information can be done with the relevance of users' information need and the value of information service to the user community. Various attempts to measure knowledge succeeded only to suggest certain ratios of measures and models. They provide mainly a ratio, ie comparative growth of information in a particular area regarding a set of publications. An exemplar of the psychometrics approach is TagueSutcliffe's construction of a measure for the informativeness of documents to readers. The value of even a simple measure of subject aboutness in the compilation of literature collections for informetric analysis was demonstrated by Wilson, who used a content-analysis approach, validated by Abstracting & Indexing services judgements.

Informetrics on the World Wide Web

The development of informetrics will be shaped considerably by the continuing technological revolution, with its shift from paper to the electronic medium. In this new realm, Harter says that "traditional bibliometric research continues on electronic documents in electronic journals using enhanced analytical power, and better facilitated by digital libraries.

In cyber metrics, web sites will play the same role as that of the documents in bibliometrics. The two important concepts that have emerged are citations (cited site) a cyber-counter part of citation and web impact factor.

The citation concepts have been applied to hypertext systems, where hypertext links between documents can be thought of as a form of reference representing an acknowledgement of the linked document. The term 'citations' has been used by Rousseau (1997) to represent a hypertext linkage between web sites, to distinguish between citations received by published works and hypertext linkages between two documents. The concept of a Web Impact Factors has been proposed by Ingwersen (1998), where the websites and its pages correspond to journals and articles respectively. This impact factor is calculated as the number of link pages pointing to a given site/domain, divided by the number of pages on a given website. Like the standard impact factor, the web impact factor serves as an indicator of website's significance. P'. While delivering Sarada Ranganathan Endowment Lecture at Institute of Information Studies, Bangalore in 1999, Egghe discussed Informetric aspects of the internet. In his presentation, he attempted to investigate the new world (virtual reality) of Internet and challenges that it offers for informetric research. Particularly, he discussed:

- The problems of data gathering
- The Internet version of the informetric laws
- Scientometric aspects of the Internet - can the clickable buttons (hyperlinks) in web pages replace the role of classical laws.
- References in journals/documents - Is there anything like web impact factor?
- Search engines in the context of information retrieval - can we apply Recall and Precision measures to evaluate search engines?
- Fractional nature of the Internet.

Obviously, in his lecture, Egghe outline the scope of the newly emerging 'webmetrics' attempt to webometrics, it may be defined as the quantitative study of web pages. New developments in informetrics concentrate more on definition and measurement of information and characteristics of retrieval performance measures and that may yield to establish a scale of measure for information logically acceptable to the field.

BIBLIOGRAMS

White (2005) in his recent article suggests the name 'bibliograms' for the distinctive core-and-scatter distributions terms studied in Informetrics, scientometrics and bibliometrics. He proposes to name it, as a way to discussing how Informetrics might be brought to wider audiences, both popular and learned. He further proposes that bibliograms are closely related to the word association lists, here called 'associagrams', long studied in Psycholinguistics and now being imported into research on thesaurus design in document retrieval. The studies that combine 'bibliograms' and associagrams' as a way of integrating Information Science and enriching it with concepts drawn from Linguistics and Psychology.

REVIEW QUESTIONS

1. Explicate the concept of informetrics.
2. Describe the use of informetrics
3. Enumerate the informetric laws
4. What are the characteristics of informetric distribution?
5. Explain the new trend in the informetrics

REFERENCE

1. Belkin, N.J., et al. (1995). Cases, scripts and information-seeking strategies: on the design of interactive information retrieval systems. Expert Systems with Applications, 9, 379- 395.
2. Blom, A. (1983). The task performance of the scientist and how it affects an information service. Mountain,3(1), 3-26.
3. Cheuk Wai-Yi, B. (1998). A piece of information seeking and using a process model in the workplace: a constructivist approach. Asian Libraries, 7(12), 375-390.
4. Cheuk Wai-Yi, B. (2000). The derivation of "situational" information seeking and use process model in the workplace: employing sense-making. Available: http://communication.sbs.ohiostate.edu/sensemaking/meet/1999/meet99cheuk.html
5. Choo, C W. (2001). Environmental scanning as information seeking and organizational learning. Information Research, 7(1).

6. Choo, C W & Auster, E. (1993). Environmental scanning: acquisition and use of information by managers. Annual Review of Information Science and Technology, 28, 279-314.
7. Choo, CW, Detlor, B & Turnbull, D. (2001). Information seeking on the Web: an integrated model of browsing and searching. First Monday, 5(2). Available: http://firstmonday.org/issues/issue 5_2/choo/index.html (Retrieved on 11.01.2016).
8. Dervin, B. (1998). Sense-making theory and practice: an overview of user interests in knowledge seeking and use. Journal of Knowledge Management, 2(2), 36-46.
9. Dervin, B. (1999.). Chaos order and sense-making: a proposed theory for information design. In Jacobson, (R E). (Ed). Information design. Cambridge, MA: MIT Press.
10. Ellis, D. (1989). A behavioural approach to information retrieval design. Journal of Documentation, 45(3), 171-212.
11. Ellis, D. and Haugan, M. (1997). Modelling the information-seeking patterns of engineers and research scientists in an industrial environment. Journal of Documentation, 53(4), 384-403.
12. Ellis, D., A. (1989). The behavioural approach to information retrieval design. Journal of Documentation, 46, 318-338.
13. Ingwersen, P. (1996). Cognitive perspectives of information retrieval interaction. Elements of a cognitive IR theory. Journal of Documentation, 52; 3-50.
14. Kuhlthau, C C. (1999). Inside the search process: information seeking from the users' perspective. Journal of the American Society for Information Science, 42 (5), 361-371.
15. Leckie, G J, Pettigrew, K E & Sylvain, C. (1996). Modelling the information seeking of professionals: a general model derived from research on engineers, health care professionals and lawyers. Library Quarterly, 66(2), 161-193.
16. Niedwiedzka, B. (2003). A proposed general model of information behaviour. Information Research, 9(1). Available: http://informationr.net/ir/9-1/paper164.html
17. Sandstrom, P E. (1994). An optimal foraging approach to information seeking and use, Library Quarterly, 64(4), 414-449.
18. Sandstorm, P E. (1999). Scholars as subsistence foragers. Bulletin of the American Society for Information Science, 25(3), 17-20.
19. Spink, A. (1997. Study of interactive feedback during mediated information retrieval. Journal of the American Society for Information Science, 8(5), 382-394.

20. Wilson, T.D. (1981). On user studies and information needs. Journal of Documentation, 37(1), 3-15.
21. Wilson, T, D. (1994). Information needs and uses: fifty years of progress? In B. C. Vickery. (Ed). Fifty years of information progress: a Journal of Documentation review. London: Aslib.
22. Wilson, T, D. and C. Walsh. (1996). Information behaviour: An Interdisciplinary perspective. Sheffield: the University of Sheffield, Department of Information Studies.
23. Wilson, T, D. (1997). Information behaviour: an interdisciplinary perspective. Information Processing and Management, 33(4), 551-572.
24. Wilson, T, D. (2000). Human information behaviour. Special issue on Information Science Research, 2(2). Available: http://inform.nu/articles/vol3/v3n2p49-56.pdf

Unit 4

OBJECTIVES
- To understand the Quantitative and Qualitative techniques
- To classify the Cluster analysis, Correspondence analysis & Coward analysis
- To study the impact of media and audience analysis
- To know about SPSS.11.0 version

4.1. INTRODUCTION

The quantitative research method aims to test pre-determined hypotheses and produce generalizable results. Using statistical methods, the results of quantitative analysis can confirm or refute hypotheses about the impact of a disaster and the ensuing needs of the affected population. They can also measure impact according to humanitarian indicators. Conclusions made from the analysis of quantitative data indicate *how many* are affected, *where* the greatest area of impact is, and *what* are the key sector needs.

4.2. QUANTITATIVE TECHNIQUES

Scientific measurement is key to quantitative research. Because quantitative data is numeric, the collection and analysis of data from representative samples are more commonly used. In its simplest terms, the more representative the sample is, the more likely it is that a quantitative analysis will accurately and precisely reflect a picture of the impact of the disaster when generalized to the whole affected population. However, even a representative sample is meaningless unless the data collection instruments used to collect quantitative data are appropriate, well designed and clearly explained to the end-users of the data. All too often, designers of data collection tools frame qualitative questions quantitatively and vice versa. Data collected using poorly designed questionnaires may solicit an enormous amount of data, but result in much of it is unusable as a result of being too difficult to measure and impossible to generalize for the total affected areas.

Larger sample sizes tend to be used for collecting quantitative information, to gather as representative a picture as possible. However, in any assessment process, there is a trade-off between the representativeness and diversity of a sample and the efficiency and timeliness with which data can be collected 5. Assessments in phase I and II do not need to be as representative as they need to be rapid6. Use of large representative sample sizes does not typically happen until phase III of an assessment when there are sufficient time and access to enable sampling of households and individuals. Previous experience in assessments highlights the fact that measurable amounts of quantitative information is often collected during assessments, but not used. This type of redundant information falls into two main question categories.

- Questions with integrity, but asked by members of an assessment team who lack the capacity and/or time to analyse the responses. For example, the question how much did you spend last week for your food? is useful, but with up to a dozen potential answers, no baseline reference to compare to, and limited resources for data analysis is too detailed to be used critically.

- Questions that are valid, but technically difficult to obtain valid answers to, given the capacities of the enumerators. For example, asking questions about MUAC measurements are likely to lead to invalid and inaccurate entries, and an eventual discounting of the data, given the expertise, experience and capacity of enumerators

4.2.1. Strengths and Weaknesses of Quantitative Research

The advantage of legitimate quantitative data, that is data which is collected rigorously, using the appropriate methods and analyzed critically, is in its reliability. However, the shortcoming of quantitative data is that it fails to provide an in-depth description of the experience of the disaster upon the affected population. Knowing how many people are affected and their locations do not provide sufficient information to guide agencies and sectors on what they should plan for in terms of response. Knowing why there is a problem and how people are affected will combine with the numbers

and locations to provide insight on how best to tailor the humanitarian response. For example, quantitative data collection may indicate categorically that 200,000 people were affected by a flood in four districts. This information would answer the questions:
- How many people have been affected by the flood?
- In how many districts?

However, this data does not tell you what priority needs are for affected persons in light of the flood or how the flood has impacted traditional coping strategies. Additional quantitative data could be collected to determine specific needs by asking community members to rank a list of priority needs. But this would still fall short of explaining *why* these are the priority needs and *how* that impacts upon and is affected by local culture and values. It would also fail to provide information about priority needs for humanitarian intervention. To gather this information, an investigator would need to ask an open-ended question, such as how has the disaster affected traditional coping strategies used by members of the community? or why are these the priority needs for your community.

The main strengths of quantitative data collection are that it provides:
- numeric estimates
- opportunity for relatively uncomplicated data analysis
- verifiable data
- data which are comparable between different communities within different locations
- data which do not require analytical judgement beyond consideration of how the information will be presented in the dissemination process.

Weaknesses inherent in quantitative data include:

Gaps in information - issues which are not included in the questionnaire, or secondary data checklist, will not be included in the analysis
- A labour-intensive data collection process
- limited participation by affected persons in the content of the questions or direction of the information collection process.

4.3. QUALITATIVE INFORMATION

Qualitative research is by definition exploratory. It is used when we don't know what to expect, how to define the issues, or lack an understanding of *why* and *how* affected populations are impacted by an emergency. Qualitative data like quantitative data is based on empiric investigation and evidence. However, qualitative research explores information from the perspective of both groups and individuals and generates case studies and summaries rather than lists of numeric data.

Qualitative data are often textual observations that portray attitudes, perceptions or intentions. Conclusions made from collected qualitative data take the form of informed assertions about the meaning and experience of certain (sub) groups of affected populations. The key contribution of qualitative data is that it provides information about the human aspect of the emergency by acknowledging context to the priority needs of affected populations and with it respecting the core principle of needs-based assistance and ownership by affected populations

4.4. QUALITATIVE RESEARCH METHODS

Qualitative methods of research and analysis provide added value in identifying and exploring intangible factors such as cultural expectations, gender roles, ethnic and religious implications and individual feelings. Qualitative research explores relationships and perceptions held by affected

persons and communities. As a result, smaller sample sizes chosen purposefully can be used for the following reasons
- The larger the sample size for qualitative data collection is, the more complex, time-consuming and multi-layered the analysis will be.
- For a truly random sample to be selected, the characteristics understudy of the whole population should be known, which is rarely possible at the early stage of an emergency.
- A random sampling of a population is likely to produce a representative sample only if the research characteristics are evenly distributed within the population. There is no evidence that the values, beliefs, attitude and perceptions that form the core of qualitative research are normally distributed, making the probability approach inappropriate.
- Some informants are more likely to provide greater insight and understanding of a disaster's impact to the assessment team, due to a variety of factors including their social, economic, educational, and cultural position in the community. Choosing someone at random to answer a qualitative question would be analogous to randomly asking a passer-by how to repair a broken car, rather than asking a garage mechanic.

The qualitative sample must be big enough to assure inclusion of most or all of the perceptions that might be important. The smaller the sample size is, the narrower the range of perceptions that may be heard. The larger the sample size, the less likely it is that the assessment team would fail to discover a perception that they would have wanted to know. In other words, the objective in designing qualitative research is to reduce the chances of discovery failure as opposed to reducing (quantitative) estimation error. In practice, the number of sample sites or groups becomes obvious as the assessment progresses, as new categories, themes and explanations stop emerging from the data (theoretical saturation). This requires a flexible assessment design and an iterative, cyclical approach to sampling, data collection, analysis and interpretation. Data gathered through qualitative methods is often presented in the form of a case study. However, as with all data, results can also be presented in graphs, tables and using other (traditionally) quantitative methods. It is important, though, to realize that just because qualitative information is presented in a graph, it does not suddenly become quantitative.

4.4.1. The main strengths of qualitative data collection are that it provides

- Rich and detailed information about affected populations
- Perspectives of specific social and cultural contexts (i.e. the human voice of the disaster)
- Inclusion of a diverse and representative cross-section of affected persons
- In-depth analysis of the impact of an emergency
- A data collection process which requires limited numbers of respondents
- A data collection process can be carried out with limited resources

(a) Weaknesses inherent in qualitative data are that it:
- Results in data which is not objectively verifiable
- Requires a labour intensive analysis process (categorization, recording, etc.)
- Needs skilled interviewers to successfully carry out the primary data collection activities.

4.5. INFERENTIAL ANALYSIS

One of the main objectives of statistical studies is to draw a valid conclusion about the population based on samples drawn from the population. Such a process of inferring about the population is called inferential analysis. The inferential analysis is often required and applied in business management. Management is confronted with various practical problems like augmentation of production, maximization of profit, minimization of cost, the introduction of innovations improvement of production methods etc. these problems lead to the accomplishment of certain pre-determined objectives and goals. There has been a growing tendency to turn to quantitative techniques as a means for solving many of these managerial decision problems that arise in a business or industrial' enterprise. A large number of business problems have been given quantitative representation with a considerable degree of success. The inferential analysis is such a quantitative e technique widely applied for managerial decision making.

The inferential analysis is a prominent quantitative technique based on probability concept to deal with uncertainty in decision making it is a set of statistical methods to assume with reasonable accuracy, population characteristics based on given in-sample statistics. Statistical inference can be defined as drawing inference from a probabilistic sample, about unknown population parameters.

The statistical inference may be focused either on examining hypotheses or on predicting probable values. Accordingly, two types of statistical inferences are hypotheses testing and statistical estimation. In hypotheses testing, we examine the claims made about unknown population parameter using sample statistics. These claims are made using some experience and logic. Statistical Estimation means estimating unknown population parameters, with reasonable accuracy, using sample statistics. This unit focuses on statistical estimation.

4.6. SIGNIFICANCE OF ESTIMATION IN MANAGERIAL DECISION MAKING

Decision making is the most important and complex task of management. Estimation is inherent in decision making. Thus, in the decision-making process, estimation plays a significant role, in the following ways.

1. Long term - the outcome of estimation will affect organizational effectiveness, for a long time. Therefore, estimates will be critical in the long run.

2. Accuracy - estimates are made based on experience and realistic projections into the future. This will ensure reasonable accuracy in estimates.

3. Goal-oriented - estimates are made, revolving around the objectives and goals of the organization. Goal orientation of estimates will improve the decision-making process.

4. Guidance - estimates are realistic projections of the future. They serve as milestones and guidance towards the attainment of vision and mission of the organization.

5. Scientific outlook - estimates and follow up will create a systematic and scientific environment within the organization. It will eliminate the rule of thumb and intuition in managerial decisions.

6. Relationship - management will have to make decisions in situations of uncertainty and risk. Statistical estimates in such situations will rationalize decisions.

4.7. SAMPLING AND SAMPLE SIZE

One of the critical factors influencing statistical estimation is a sampling. Sampling is reliable to study the whole population. A housewife takes a few rice, from a boiling pot, to check its cooling. She is ensuring the cooking of the whole pot. Sampling is a tool which helps to know the characteristics of the population. Sampling is defined as the process of drawing a representative number of items for collecting information to infer about the population.

Several sampling techniques or methods are in use to get the required data. They are broadly classified as random sampling techniques and nonrandom sampling techniques. Random sampling techniques include simple random sampling, stratified sampling, systematic sampling and cluster sampling etc. non-random sampling techniques include judgment sampling, multistage sampling, quota sampling, snowball sampling etc.

(a) **Simple random sampling:** This is the easiest method of sampling. In this technique, every item gets an opportunity of being selected. This technique is applied by taking lots or Random Number Tables. B.

(b) **Stratified random sampling :** Here the population is subdivided into several strata of homogenous items. Then samples are taken from each stratum to make up the total number of samples.

(c) **Systematic sampling :** Under this technique, the researcher follows a system of rules for selecting the required samples.

(d) **Cluster sampling:** Here the population is located in convenient clusters where items concentrate Required sample numbers are selected from such clusters, applying some random technique.

(e) **Judgment sampling :** Here samples are taken according to judgment or purpose. We simply pick those items which convenient to select.

(f) **Multistage sampling:** The population is subdivided into several stages from top to bottom and the lowest stage is utilized for sample selection.

(e) **Quota sampling:** Here quotas are fixed, and required sample numbers are picked according to the quota determined.

(g) Snowball sampling : This is a type of convenient sampling technique, where initially a few items are selected samples, and as the study proceeds, required sample numbers are added according to convenience.

4.7.1. Sample size

The sample size is the number of items included in a sample. This is a decisive factor in accurately estimating population parameters. Sampling precision depends more on sample size, and not on the proportion of the population sampled. In sampling analysis, vital questions are - how large the sample should be? If the sample size is too small; estimation may be inaccurate. If it is too large, the heavy cost may be incurred.

4.8. FACTORS INFLUENCING SAMPLE SIZE

As a general rule, the sample must be of an optimum size. Size of the sample is determined by the following factors.

1. Nature of population : Population may be homogenous or heterogeneous. If it is homogenous, a small sample can serve the purpose. Otherwise, a large sample is required.

2. Nature of study : if the intensive and focused study is required, a small sample will do. For a general study, large samples may be undertaken.

3. Sampling technique : sampling technique plays an important role in sample size. A small but the properly selected sample is better than a large but poorly selected sample.

4. Accuracy : If a higher level of accuracy is required, relatively larger samples are required. For doubling the level of accuracy, the sample size should be increased fourfold.

4.8.1. Approaches in sample size decision

There are two alternative approaches for determining the size of the sample. The first approach is to specify the precision of estimation desired and then to determine sample size (n) necessary to ensure it. The second approach uses the cost of additional information against the expected value of additional information. The first approach is capable of solving a mathematical solution, and as such is a frequently used technique of determining sample size.

The limitation of this technique is that it does not consider the cost of gathering information. The second approach is theoretically optimal but is rarely used because of difficulty in measuring the value of information. Therefore, we shall concentrate here on the first approach.

4.8.2. Determining sample size -confidence level approach

When a sample study is made, sampling errors are bound to occur, and this can be controlled by selecting a sample of adequate size. The precision level must be specified along with confidence level. Sample size can be determined considering such level of confidence, standard deviation and expected error.

4.9. TESTS OF SIGNIFICANCE - CONCEPTS

One of the objectives of statistical investigation is to evaluate whether there is a significant difference between the estimated parameter and true parameter after estimating population mean or proportion. Naturally, a question arises - Does the estimated parameter conform to the real parameter, or, is there any considerable difference between them, the answer leads us to the evaluation of difference. There are tests to assess the significance of such difference, which are called significance tests.

The basis of statistical tests is a hypothesis. First, we form a hypothesis regarding the population. Then we conduct a test to ass whether there is any significant, difference. The hypothesis will be accepted or rejected according to the significance of the difference revealed by the test. Therefore, a significance test is also called hypothesis tests. In social sciences where direct knowledge of population parameter is rare, significance or hypothesis testing is the often-used strategy for deciding whether sample data support population characteristics or not.

(a) Basic concepts : Significance tests are amply supported by several theoretical basic concepts. To conduct tests, knowledge of following basic ingredients are essential.

(b) Types of significance tests : There are numerous types of significance tests, according to situations and criteria of testing. Tests may be parametrical or non-parametric, one-tailed or two-tailed, small sample or large sample etc.

4.10. PARAMETRIC AND NON-PARAMETRIC TESTS

Based on the focus of the test, they can be classified as a parametric and non-parametric test. In certain tests, the assumption about population distribution can be made. For example, in a large sample test or Z test, we assume that samples are drawn from the population following a normal distribution. Such tests which are based on assumptions about population are called parametric tests. Mean Tests, Proportion Tests, Variance tests are parametric tests. These tests focus on means of samples or population, proportion, variance or standard deviation and accordingly, all mean tests, proportion tests or variance tests are parametric tests.

But in certain situations, it is not possible to make any assumption about population distribution, from which samples are drawn. Besides they do not focus on parameters like mean, the proportion of variance. Such tests are called non-parametric tests. Non-parametric tests include Chi-square test. Rank test. Sign test, Runs test etc.

4.11. SMALL SAMPLE AND LARGE SAMPLE TESTS

According to the number of items included in a sample,

tests can be divided as small sample tests and large sample tests. If the test includes a sample of size less than 30, it is a small sample test. If the size is 30 or more, it is a large sample test. Small sample tests follow the student's t distribution. Large samples tests follow the normal distribution. Mean tests may be conducted as large or small tests. But proportions are conducted as large sample tests only.

4.12. ONE-TAILED OR TWO-TAILED TESTS

Based on the location of the rejection region, tests may be one-tailed or two-tailed. When a test examines the significance of the difference of either more than a specific value or less than a specific value, rejection appears only on one side of the curve. It is called a one-tailed test.

4.13. HYPOTHESIS

A hypothesis is the basis of all significance tests. For a researcher, it is a formal question that he intends to resolve. Usually, we begin some assumptions about the population from which the sample is drawn. This assumption may be about the form of the population or the parameters of the population. Such an assumption is called the hypothesis.

A hypothesis may be defined as "a tentative conclusion logically drawn concerning the parameter or the form of the distribution of the population. Example of hypothesis may be "the mean of the population will be 12000" or "the population proportion will be the same as the sample proportion."

4.13.1. Types of hypotheses

According to nature and situation, the hypothesis may be simple or composite, parametric and non-parametric, null or alternative.

(a) Simple and composite hypothesis : If a hypothesis is concerning sample statistic or population parameter only, it is called a simple hypothesis. For example, "population standard deviation conforms to sample standard deviation" is a simple hypothesis." If a hypothesis forms a statement about any sample statistic or parameter and form of distribution, it is called a composite hypothesis. For example, "population follows the normal distribution with mean = 25" is a composite hypothesis."

(b) Parametric and non-parametric hypothesis : A hypothesis which specifies only the parameter or statistic of either the sample or population is called a parametric hypothesis. If a hypothesis specifies only the form of the distribution, it is non-parametric. For example, the hypothesis "Mean of the population is 2300" is a parametric hypothesis, while "population-is normal" is non-parametric.

(c) The null and alternative hypothesis : A null hypothesis is a statistical hypothesis which states that the difference between the sample statistic or population parameter is nil, or statistically insignificant. Usually, null hypotheses are formed for significance testing. Any hypothesis other than the null hypothesis is called an alternative hypothesis. The null hypothesis is denoted by Ho and alternative hypothesis by HI, H2 and so on.

4.14. MULTIDIMENSIONAL SCALING

Multidimensional scaling is a visual representation of distances or dissimilarities between sets of objects. "Objects" can be colours, faces, map coordinates, political persuasion, or any kind of real or conceptual stimuli (Kruskal and Wish, 1978). Objects that are more similar (or have shorter distances) are closer together on the graph than objects that are less similar (or have longer distances). As well as interpreting dissimilarities as distances on a graph, MDS can also serve as a dimension reduction technique for high-dimensional data (Buja et. al, 2007).

The term scaling comes from *psychometrics*, where abstract concepts ("objects") are assigned numbers according to a rule (Trochim, 2006). For example, you may want to quantify a person's attitude to global warming. You could assign a "1" to "doesn't believe in global warming", a 10 to "firmly believes in global warming" and a scale of 2 to 9 for attitudes in between. You can also think of "scaling" as the fact that you're essentially *scaling down the data* (i.e. making it simpler by creating lower-dimensional data). Data that is scaled down in dimension keeps similar properties. For example, two data points that are close together in *high-dimensional* space will also be close together in low-dimensional space (Martinez, 2005). The **"multidimensional"** part is since you aren't limited to two-dimensional graphs or data. Three-dimensional, four-dimensional and higher plots are possible.

MDS is now used over a wide variety of disciplines. Its use isn't limited to a specific matrix or set of data; In fact, just about any matrix can be analyzed with the technique as long as the matrix contains some type of relational data (Young, 2013). Examples of relational data include *correlations*, distances, multiple rating scales or similarities. As you may be able to tell from the short discussion above, MDS is very difficult to understand unless you have a basic understanding of matrix algebra and dimensionality. If you're new to this concept, you may want to read these articles first

4.15. CLUSTER ANALYSIS

The objective of cluster analysis is to assign observations to groups (\clusters") so that observations within each group are similar to one another concerning variables or attributes of interest, and the groups themselves stand apart from one another. In other words, the objective is to divide the observations into homogeneous and distinct groups. In contrast to the classification problem here each observation is known to belong to one of some groups and the objective is to predict the group to which a new observation belongs, cluster analysis seeks to discover the number and composition of the groups. There are some clustering methods. One method, for example, begins with as many groups as there are observations, and then systematically merges observations to reduce the number of groups by one, two,::::, until a single group containing all observations is formed. Another method begins with a given number of groups and an arbitrary assignment of the observations to the groups and then reassigns the observations one by one so that ultimately each observation belongs to the nearest group.

Cluster analysis is also used to group variables into homogeneous and distinct groups. This approach is used, for example, in revising a questionnaire based on responses received to a draft of the questionnaire. The grouping of the questions employing cluster analysis helps to identify redundant questions and reduce their number, thus improving the chances of a good response rate to the final version of the questionnaire.

Cluster analysis embraces a variety of techniques, the main objective of which is to group observations or variables into homogeneous and distinct clusters. A simple numerical example will help explain these objectives.

Example 4.1 The daily expenditures on food (X1) and clothing (X2) of five persons are shown in Table 4.1.

Table 4.1. Illustrative data of Example 4.1.

Sl.No	Person	X_1	X_2
1.	a	2	4
2.	b	8	2
3.	c	9	5
4.	d	1	3
5.	e	8.5	1

The numbers are fictitious and not at all realistic, but the example will help us explain the essential features of cluster analysis as simple as possible. The data of Table 15.1 are plotted in Figure 4.1.

A Textbook of User Studies and Informetrics   155

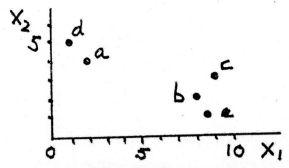

Fig. 4.1. Grouping of observations, Example 4.1

Inspection of Figure 4.1 suggests that the positive observations form two clusters. The rst consists of persons a and d, and the second of b, c and e. It can be noted that the observations in each cluster are similar to one another concerning expenditures on food and clothing and that the two clusters are quite distinct from each other. These conclusions concerning the number of clusters and their membership were reached through a visual inspection of Figure 4.1. This inspection was possible because only two variables were involved in grouping the observations. The question is: Can a procedure be devised for similarly grouping observations when there are more than two variables or attributes.

A straightforward procedure may be to examine all possible clusters of the available observations and to summarize each clustering according to the degree of proximity among the cluster elements and of the separation among the clusters. Unfortunately, this is not feasible because in most cases in practice the number of all possible clusters is very large and out of reach of current computers. Cluster analysis offers several methods that operate much as a person would in attempting to reach systematically a reasonable grouping of observations or variables.

4.16. MEASURES OF DISTANCE FOR VARIABLES

Clustering methods require a more precise definition of

\similarity" (\closeness", proximity") of observations and clusters. When the grouping is based on variables, it is natural to employ the familiar concept of distance. Consider Figure 15.2 as a map showing two points, i and j, with coordinates (X1i; X2i) and (X1j; X2j), respectively

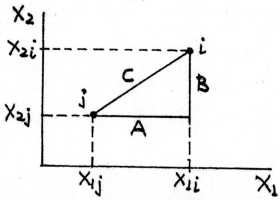

Fig. 4.2. Distance measures illustrated

4.17. CLUSTERING METHODS

Given a distance measure, a reasonable procedure for grouping n observations proceeds in the following steps. Begin with as many clusters as there are observations, that is, with each observation forming a separate cluster. Merge that pair of observations that are nearest one another, leaving n ¡ 1 clusters for the next step. Next, merge into one cluster that pair of clusters that are nearest one another, leaving n ¡ 2 clusters for the next step. Continue in this fashion, reducing the number of clusters by one at each step, until a single cluster is formed consisting of all n observations. At each step, keep track of the distance at which the clusters are formed. To determine the number of clusters, consider the step(s) at which the merging distance is relatively large. A problem with this procedure is how to measure the distance between clusters consisting of two or more observations. Perhaps the simplest method is to treat the distance between the two nearest observations, one from each cluster, as the distance between the two clusters. This is known as the nearest neighbour (or single linkage) method

Fig. 4.3. Cluster distance, nearest neighbour method

(a) Hierarchical agglomerative methods

Within this approach to cluster analysis, there are several different methods used to determine which clusters should be joined at each stage. The main methods are summarised below.

Nearest neighbour method (single linkage method): In this method, the distance between two clusters is defined to be the distance between the two closest members, or neighbours. This method is relatively simple but is often criticized because it doesn't take account of cluster structure and can result in a problem called chaining whereby clusters end up being long and straggly. However, it is better than the other methods when the natural clusters are not spherical or elliptical.

(b) Furthest neighbour method (complete linkage method)

In this case, the distance between two clusters is defined to be the maximum distance between members — i.e. the distance between the two subjects that are furthest apart.

This method tends to produce compact clusters of similar size but, as for the nearest neighbour method, does not take account of cluster structure. It is also quite sensitive to outliers.

(c) Average (between groups) linkage method (sometimes referred to as UPGMA)

The distance between two clusters is calculated as the average distance between all pairs of subjects in the two clusters. This is considered to be a fairly robust method.

(d) Centroid method

Here the centroid (mean value for each variable) of each cluster is calculated and the distance between centroids is used. Clusters whose centroids are closest together are merged. This method is also fairly robust.

(e) Ward's method

In this method, all possible pairs of clusters are combined and the sum of the squared distances within each cluster is calculated. This is then summed over all clusters. The combination that gives the lowest sum of squares is chosen. This method tends to produce clusters of approximately equal size, which is not always desirable. It is also quite sensitive to outliers. Despite this, it is one of the most popular methods, along with the average linkage method. It is generally a good idea to try two or three of the above methods. If the methods agree reasonably well then the results will be that much more believable.

4.18. SELECTING THE OPTIMUM NUMBER OF CLUSTERS

As stated above, once the cluster analysis has been carried out it is then necessary to select the 'best' cluster solution. There are some ways in which this can be done, some rather informal and subjective, and some more formal. The more formal methods will not be discussed in this handout. Below, one of the informal methods is briefly described. When carrying out a hierarchical cluster analysis, the process can be represented on a diagram known as a dendrogram. This diagram illustrates which clusters have been joined at each stage of the analysis and the distance between clusters at the time of joining. If there is a large jump in the distance between clusters from one stage to another then this suggests that at one stage clusters that are relatively close together were joined whereas, at the following stage, the clusters that were joined were relatively far apart. This implies that the optimum number of clusters may be the number present just before that large jump in distance.

4.19. NON-HIERARCHICAL OR K-MEANS CLUSTERING METHODS

In these methods, the desired number of clusters is specified in advance and the 'best' solution is chosen. The steps in such a method are as follows:

1. Choose initial cluster centres (essentially this is a set of observations that are far apart — each subject forms a cluster of one and its centre is the value of the variables for that subject).
2. Assign each subject to its 'nearest' cluster, defined in terms of the distance to the centroid.
3. Find the centroids of the clusters that have been formed
4. Re-calculate the distance from each subject to each centroid and move observations that are not in the cluster that they are closest to.
5. Continue until the centroids remain relatively stable.

Non-hierarchical cluster analysis tends to be used when large data sets are involved. It is sometimes preferred because it allows subjects to move from one cluster to another (this is not possible in hierarchical cluster analysis where a subject, once assigned, cannot move to a different cluster). Two disadvantages of non-hierarchical cluster analysis are: (1) it is often difficult to know how many clusters you are likely to have and therefore the analysis may have to be repeated several times and (2) it can be very sensitive to the choice of initial cluster centres. Again, it may be worth trying different ones to see what impact this has. One possible strategy to adopt is to use a hierarchical approach initially to determine how many clusters there are in the data and then to use the cluster centres obtained from this as initial cluster centres in the non-hierarchical method.

4.20. CORRESPONDENCE ANALYSIS

Correspondence analysis is a multivariate exploratory space reduction technique for categorical data analysis. Although certainly true, such a description tells the linguist little. Equally true, but perhaps more helpful, is to describe correspondence analysis as an exploratory technique that reveals frequency-based associations in corpus data. Most importantly, perhaps, the technique visualizes these associations to facilitate their identification. Linguists often wish to find relations between given linguistic forms, between their meanings and in what situations those forms and meanings are used. Correspondence analysis is specially designed for identifying such usage patterning. The visualization of the relations takes the form of configuration biplots, or maps, which depict degrees of correlation and variation through the relative proximity of data points (which represent linguistic usage features and/or the actual examples of use). This paper describes how to perform correspondence analysis in R. It explains the R code needed to execute the analyses and shows how to interpret the results.

4.21. USE OF CORRESPONDENCE ANALYSIS

In their quotidian research, linguists, from all kinds of theoretical orientations, analyse various usage-features of naturally occurring utterances. By way of example, imagine that one obtains 600 examples of a given word, a grammatical case, or a syntactic pattern. These examples can then be analyzed, using traditional intuition-based analysis for a range of usage-features, such as tense, aspect, argument structure, agent type, the ground or path type, and the register or genre from which the example is taken. The results of analysing the examples for these usage-features can be summarised as counts of how often each of the features occurs. Significance tests can then be used to show that the occurrence of certain features is substantially more common than could be expected by chance. This statistically significant variation can then, in turn, be interpreted as representing a distinct pattern of usage. However, with more than a couple of different dimensions of analysis or large numbers of features at play, interpreting the numbers of occurrences becomes increasingly difficult, if not impossible. Quite simply, correspondence analysis is an exploratory tool that helps one find which usage-features co-occur with other usage-features, giving a map of their overall patterning. Assuming that one is adopting a cognitive or functional approach to language, these usage-patterns can be interpreted as grammatical description, operationalized in terms of relative frequency.

It must be stressed that this technique is designed solely for exploratory purposes. In other words, it is a tool for finding things, not for establishing their significance or discerning their relevance. Therefore, it offers you no assurance that patterns found are anything more than a chance result, specific to the sample under observation. Moreover, this tool does not tell you where to look. Although exploratory, one must avoid 'fishing' for results by randomly combining factors in the hope of finding correlations that could be interpretable. Even if one finds correlations that 'make sense', such an approach increases the chance of finding co-incidental correlations or chance patterns in the sample. A metaphor that might be helpful is that of the shovel for the archaeologist: if one digs randomly, everywhere, it increases the chances of finding irrelevant things. Correspondence analysis is a tool for digging in the data for patterns and correlations. Yet the metaphor can still serve us further: when an archaeologist finds an artefact, it is still up to the archaeologist to interpret the finding as well as to verify its authenticity. Correspondence analysis, assuming you have a reasonable hypothesis about where to look, is a basic and useful tool for unearthing patterns in the data, but it is no more than that.

4.21.1. Concept of correspondence analysis

Correspondence analysis takes the frequency of co-occurring features and converts them to distances, which are then plotted, revealing how things are related by how close to or far from each other they are in a two- or three-dimensional visualization. In the detail, there is much more to the technique, but this is the principle. Explaining a few key concepts will allow us to better understand the functioning of the technique as well as to interpret its results.

(a) Distance Matrix : The distance matrix is sometimes also called a proximity matrix and even a dissimilarity matrix. The concept is simple: the frequencies of co-occurrence are converted to distances. The resulting distance matrix can then be visualised in a two- or three-dimensional Euclidean space ('normal' perceptual space). More precisely, it is the differences between the rows and columns of frequencies that are converted to distances. Correspondence analysis uses the chi-square distance measure to produce the distance matrix. This measure is designed to compensate for different 'amounts' of a given category. In other words, if one has only a few examples of a given feature, let us say the 'future tense', it is highly likely that they will all, or mostly, co-occur with some other feature, such as a given verb. However, due to the low numbers involved, this is much more likely to be chance than other correlations identified. The chi-square distance measure attempts to compensate for this kind of bias. Nevertheless, despite the use of the chi-square measure, with experience, one will still observe (in the plots) correlations that are likely to be due to small numbers of a given feature. It is always necessary to go back to both the data, that is the actual language examples, and to the raw frequencies, to see what the plots have 'revealed'. Greencare offers a lucid explanation of the chi-square distance measure. Euclidean cloud The distance matrix takes the form of a Euclidean cloud. In other words, it is a spread of points in a given space, like rice thrown onto a board or the holes made by darts on a dartboard. Correspondence analysis computes the Eigenvectors of a correlation matrix and produces this Euclidean 'map', in one or two dimensions of that correlation. It can be thought of as reducing a set of Chi-square scores to Euclidean distances (natural perceptual distances), suitable for two- or three-dimension visualizations. For the reader familiar with exploratory statistics, it is essentially the same as principal components analysis but modified for categorical data.

(b) Profiles and mass : A profile is the behavioural characteristics of a given category in the analysis, determined by the set of relative co-occurrence frequencies of that category. In a frequency (contingency) table, it is a column or a row containing all the relative frequencies of those co-occurrences. It is these profiles that the correspondence analysis plots. To calculate the profile, you add the number of occurrences for each feature in a row. You then divide each of those occurrences by the sum of them. This gives you a profile figure for each cell. The same procedure is undertaken for the columns, giving you the column profiles. However, as mentioned above, not all co-occurrences are of equal importance. Infrequent features would have a disproportionate effect if all were taken equally. Correspondence analysis uses weighted averages of the profiles to compensate for this. In correspondence analysis, the term 'mass' is used to mean 'weight'. Weighing an average modifies the calculation to bias certain scores. It is widely used in basic statistics, from calculating the average score in a class test to the average monthly profit of a franchised shop. Inertia and Variation The higher the explained inertia one obtains, the better. Inertia is the term used in correspondence analysis to talk about the degree of variation. The inertia is calculated on observed and expected frequencies of co-occurrence. Inertia is high when column and row profiles have large deviations from their averages. In multiple correspondence analysis (as opposed to binary correspondence analysis), these scores are not interpretable, which is a major drawback for this form of the technique. They are not interpretable because the scores calculated seriously under-estimate the amount of accurately described variation, giving unnecessarily 'bad' results. Two corrections to this have been proposed, firstly by the original author of the technique, Benzécri [reported in Greencare 2006: 68]), and secondly by the current main proponent of the technique, Greencare (2006: 68). Greencare argues that Benzécri's original correction was biased towards an overly optimistic result, that is, explaining more variation than was the case. The {ca} package, described in section 2.3.2, includes an option to apply Greencare's inertia adjustment. Its application is explained in section 2.3.2.

(c) **Biplots** : The concept behind the visualization in a biplot is quite simple to understand. The correspondence analysis has calculated proximity values for the combination of the cells across the rows and columns of a contingency table. These can be plotted. Each dimension of the plot (there are two dimensions in a biplot) will explain a certain percentage of the data variation, or 'inertia'. Plotting a single dimension, a simple line or the x-axis will place the data points on this line at varying distances from each other. However, in most situations, this will poorly represent the relations between those features. If we add a second dimension, the y-axis, we obtain a two-dimensional biplot, typical of correspondence analysis and a range of other space reduction techniques. This will, hopefully, explain a great deal of the variation in the data. The scores of the explained inertia (or variation) are typically given for these first two axes. Although, theoretically, it is possible to take any two dimensions and plot these. Normally, a combination of the first two dimensions captures a large percentage of the variation. Adding a third dimension, the z-axis produces a three-dimensional plot that will even more accurately represent the behaviour of the data. Three-dimensional plots are also possible in R but are not considered in this discussion.

Sometimes, it is useful to examine combinations of dimensions one and three or even two and three in biplots, especially when the explained inertia is low. For most data sets, though, a combination of the first two dimensions offers the most accurate and interpretable visualisation of the variation and association in the data. The numerical summary of a correspondence analysis will list all the dimensions, but above the third- or fourth dimension, further dimensions rarely represent anything more than a small fraction of the variation. To completely represent a contingency table, one would need all the dimensions. The number of possible dimensions is equal to the number of rows or columns (whichever is smaller) minus one. So, to visualize a table with five rows and eight columns, one would need four dimensions. Unfortunately, there is a range of terminology that varies from one book to another and even from one R package to the next. A few basic terms that may arise, especially in the numerical summaries of the analysis include 'Eigenvalues', which indicates the inertia; the 'percentages of explained variance', or simply the percentage of inertia; and 'communalities', which are the percentages of explained inertia for individual rows or columns. If one wishes to work with the technique, three excellent books clearly explain its functioning, accessible even to readers with no statistical training.

4.22. BINARY AND MULTIPLE CORRESPONDENCE ANALYSIS

Correspondence analysis is, in fact, a family of techniques and a family that is growing. There exist at least three kinds of binary correspondence analysis and three kinds of multiple correspondence analysis. Binary correspondence analysis can be understood as the basis for the multiple correspondence analysis. It has two advantages over the latter. Firstly, it indicates the percentage of explained inertia for each axis. This tells you how well your analysis fits the data (how much of the variation the analysis captures). It is even possible to add confidence ellipses that estimate statistical significance (see section 2.4.1). Secondly, the plots are simpler to interpret, which is an extremely important advantage.

On the other hand, the advantage of multiple correspondence analysis is that you can add more than two factors. The ability to capture the interaction of more than two different factors should not be underrated. In linguistics, lexical structure, syntactic structure, prosodic structure, argument structure, as well as region, gender, register and so on, are all potentially and interdependently relevant in language structure and its description.

Although combining factors in this manner will permit us to perform cluster analysis and binary correspondence analysis is restricted to 'normal' two-way tables). In the R sessions below, we consider three kinds – indicator matrix multiple correspondence analysis, Burt matrix multiple correspondence analysis, and joint multiple correspondence analysis.

Indicator multiple correspondence analysis is sometimes called homogeneity analysis (Gifi 1990, De Leeuw & Mair 2009a). It uses a 'binary matrix of indicators' (dummy variables) to 'combine' the binary correspondence analyses. Despite mathematical differences, its results are very similar to Burt matrix multiple correspondence analysis. Indeed, Greenacre (2007: 141) compares the two and concludes that there is no difference in the visualisation of the results, but that the Burt matrix produces more 'optimistic' percentages of inertia. However, for multiple correspondence analysis, it must be remembered that the percentages of explained inertia cannot be interpreted because they severely underestimate the representative quality of the biplot map. Nevertheless, the Burt matrix multiple correspondence analysis is the most commonly implemented in R and what we will employ here. The third type of multiple correspondence analysis is based on the Burt matrix method and has been termed joint correspondence analysis. Greencare (2006: 68; 2007: 145) argues that it is superior both in terms of the explained inertia and in the accuracy of the visualisation. It works by restricting the analysis to the cross-tabulations that typically contain the correlations of interest, those that explain the inertia. Greencare (2007: ch. 19) explains the technique in clear terms.

4.23. PERFORMING AND INTERPRETING CORRESPONDENCE ANALYSIS IN R

Before we begin with the application *per se*, we must cover a few general questions that are relevant to every correspondence analysis. The first important question is – what to look for. There are four issues: 'fishing', over simplicity, over-complexity, and data sparseness. Let us briefly consider each in turn. By fishing, we mean the arbitrary (or near-arbitrary) selection of factors in the hope that one will find correlations. Correspondence analysis is a tool for identifying correlations, a tool that needs to be used in a reasoned fashion. There is no point in establishing correlations between the use of language features that bear no interpretable correlation in reality, or worse, bear an interpretable correlation, but are just a result of few a chance occurrence. In section 1.1, the metaphor of an archaeologist digging was used to explain this point: by digging everywhere, it is sure that something will be found, but the chances of finding irrelevant things increase exponentially. Over-simplicity is less serious a problem, but still must be borne in mind.

There is no use in using correspondence analysis to identify a correlation that a simple pie chart or histogram, combined with a significance test, would do even better. Similarly, obvious correlations can dominate results at the expense of less obvious, and therefore, more interesting results. For example, in the case of a correlation between first person singular uses of a mental predicate and parenthetical uses of a mental predicate – since the vast majority all parenthetical uses will be in the first person, entering these factors (grammatical person and parenthetically) will reveal an obvious correlation.

The problem is, if these two factors are amongst a more complex range of factors, the obvious correlation could 'override', or 'hide', other correlations. Although it is sometimes necessary to leave such obvious correlations in the analysis because one is seeking structures in other parts of the data, if it is possible to avoid doing so, then it should be avoided. Obvious correlations run the risk of 'hiding' the more interesting results. In other words, the plot will identify what is most strongly correlated instead of the subtler, yet analytically more important correlations. Over-complexity occurs in binary correspondence analysis when using concatenated tables (see section 2.2.3 below) and in a multiple correspondence analysis when too many factors are examined simultaneously. For example, there is no point analysing, simultaneously, 22 factors, each with 16 features, even if one has thousands of examples. Without even considering the impossibility of accounting for the variation (inertia), in such a dataset, the results would not be interpretable for the simple reason that the visualisation of so many factors become impossible to decipher. Moreover, the chance of 'false' associations increases dramatically with the more variables and features that are considered simultaneously. There is no steadfast rule, but thinking about how the analysis works and being realistic about its limitations are the safest ways to avoid the problem of over-complexity. One way to avoid such over-complexity is to work with subsets. Subsets may be logical divisions within the data: for example, examining two dialects independently from one another or examining two lexemes or grammatical constructions separately. Similarly, certain features or factors can be combined. As long as the choice is reasoned and reported, it can help to simplify the interactions that the analysis is trying to explain. This principle extends to data sparseness and 'small cells'. As a rule of thumb, one aims to have at least ten examples in each cell of the cross-tabulated matrix (see below, this section). This is not always possible, but cells of less than eight tend to cause distortions in the analysis. One may find that the analysis is 'trying so hard' to account for some relatively infrequent use, that the important associations are not represented. A response to this problem is to leave out the examples (the rows in a flat data-frame, see below, this section) that contribute features only occurring a few times. First performing the correspondence analysis on the full set of data and then gradually taking out these small cells (rows of infrequent examples) is a good heuristic. Not only will it result in a better final analysis, but the exploratory nature of correspondence analysis will also help you to better understand the data and the correlations within them. The numerical output of binary correspondence analysis can be very helpful in identifying such problems. Using the numerical output, one can quickly see which data points are being poorly represented. This is explained in section 2.3.1. Let us now turn to the computation and interpretation of correspondence analysis in R. Some common packages for correspondence analysis include: {MASS}, {ca}, {languageR}, {anacor}, {homals}, {FactoMineR}, {vegan}, {ade4} and {pamctdp}. Unfortunately, for reasons of brevity, we restrict the demonstration to a small selection of functionalities in the first four of these packages. However, references to further information and tutorials on each is offered.

Each package is a suite of commands for performing correspondence analysis. They have different options and possibilities. The program R works with functions, such as the function to read a table, to plot results of an analysis and, of course, to perform statistical analysis. In simple terms, the functions are the commands that tell R what to do. Each function also has a set of 'arguments'. These arguments are the 'options' that R should take into account in executing the command. They should be carefully typed – spaces do not affect, but capitals commas, brackets, and so forth must be entered exactly. Moreover, keeping a record of what you have done is vital in learning to use the program. There are lots of additions in R for keeping your working history and also for storing the functions you use often. However, when just beginning, it is perhaps simplest, to use a text file and to simply 'copy' and 'paste' to and from R. Also at the end of an R session, it is wise to save the history (what you have done) either within R or in a separate text file. This will help you to remember the steps you took the next time you perform an analysis.

In the R sessions below, after each line of command, another short line is added, following the # sign. This sign indicates that the program R should ignore what follows it and not try to interpret it as arguments belonging to the function. It is standard practice to explain command lines after such hash (#) signs. To explain how to perform and interpret the analyses in R, we will use artificial data. Let us take a range of near-synonymous verbs in an imaginary language. In this language, let us say, there are three mental predicates think, believe, and suppose, and three communication predicates, say, speak, and talk, which can be used figuratively to also indicate epistemic stance, just like the mental predicates. We take 575 occurrences of the verbs, more or less equally distributed. Correspondence analysis does not require equal distribution in such a situation, but we want to have as many examples as possible of each form, so making a balanced selection fulfils this requirement. The imaginary language possesses a three-way distinction in the aspect mood system, distinguishing between 'Perfective', 'Imperfective' and 'Modal' forms. Each of the examples is analyzed for this grammatical category. The examples are also analyzed for the grammatical person of the verb and the semantic type of the indirect object.

4.24. MEDIA AND AUDIENCE ANALYSIS

We all know that mass communication is a process of sharing messages to a large number of audiences through some forms of technology at a time. And some forms of technology used to spread messages in the media.

(a) **Information**: Sending and sharing of information is the major function of media. Since information is knowledge and knowledge is power, media offer authentic and timely facts and opinions about various event and situations to a mass audience as informative items. Information provided by mass media can be opinionated, objective, subjective, primary and secondary. Informative functions of media also let the audience knows about the happening around them and come to the truth. Media disseminates information mostly through a news broadcast on radio, TV, as well as columns of the newspaper or magazines.

(b) **Education** : Media provides education and information. It provides education in different subjects to people of all levels. They try to educate people directly or indirectly using different forms of content. For example, a distance education program is a direct approach. Dramas, documentaries, interviews, feature stories and many other programs are prepared to educate people indirectly. Especially in the developing country, mass media is used as effective tools for mass awareness.

(c) **Entertainment** : The other important function of media is entertainment. It is also viewed as the most obvious and often used function of media. Entertainment is a kind of performance that pleasures people. Media fulfil this function by amusing people. Newspaper and magazines, radio, television and online medium offer stories, films, serials, and comics to entertain their audience. Sports, news, film review, art and fashion are other examples. It makes the audience recreational and leisure time more enjoyable and fun.

(d) **Persuasion** : It is another function of mass media. Persuasion involves making an influence on others mind. Mass media influence audience in varieties of ways. Media content builds opinions and sets agendas in the public mind. It influences votes, changes attitudes and moderates behaviour. Using editorials, articles, commentaries and among others, mass media persuades the audience. However, all audiences are not well known about it. Many of them become influenced or motivated unknowingly towards it. Advertisement is the example which is designed to persuade.

(e) Surveillance : Surveillance denotes observation. Here observation means to watch the society closely. The function of mass media is to observe the society closely and continuously and warn about threatening actions to the mass audience that is likely to happen in future to decrease the possible loss. Likewise, mass media also informs about the misconducts happening in the society to the concerned authority and discourage malpractices among the mass audience in the society. Warning or beware surveillance occurs when the media. inform us about threats from hurricanes, erupting volcanoes, depressed economic conditions, increasing inflation or military attack. These warning can be about immediate threats or chronic threats. Similarly, news of increasing deforestation, drug abuse, girls trafficking, crimes etc. are also disseminated which may harm the peace and security of the society. News about films are plying at the local theatres, stock market prices, new products, fashion ideas, recipes, and so on are examples of instrumental surveillance.

(f) Interpretation : The mass media do not supply just facts and data but also explanations and interpretation of events and situations. Media offer various explanations correlating and interpreting information to make the reality clear. Unlike normal reporting, interpretation functions provide knowledge. News analysis, commentaries, editorials, and columns are some examples of interpretative contents.

(g) Linkage : The function of media is to join together different elements of society that are not directly connected. For instance: mass advertising attempts to link the needs of buyers with the products of sellers. In this way, media become a bridge between different groups who may or may not have a direct connection.

(h) Socialization : Socialization is the transmission of culture. Media are the reflectors of society. They socialize people, especially children and new-comers. Socialization is a process by which, people are made to behave in ways that are acceptable in their culture or society. Through this process, we learn how to become a member of our society or human society in a greater sense. Though the process of socialization media helps to shape our behaviours, conducts, attitudes and beliefs. The process of socialization brings people close and ties them into a single unity.

Media today consists of television, the Internet, cinema, newspapers, radio, magazines, direct mail, fax, and the telephone. Viewers can see some pictorial representation of messages through different types of broadcasting and advertising. Images are visual representations, pictures, graphics, and include video, movies. Images are very useful in media to help share messages effectively.

Nowadays, our life will be incomplete without media. It provides an easy way of communication where people can contact friends and family from any location of the world. At the same time, media like television, radio and the Internet enhance our knowledge by providing access to information from all over the world.

4.25. CATEGORIES OF MEDIA

The term news media refers to the groups that communicate information and news to people. There are three main categories of media: print media, broadcast media, and New Media.

(a) Print Media

The term 'print media' is used to describe the traditional or "old-fashioned" print-based media that today's parents grew up with, including newspapers, magazines, books, and comics or graphic novels. Historically, only wealthy publishers had access to sophisticated type-setting technologies necessary to create printed material, but this has changed in recent years with the widespread accessibility of desktop publishing software and print-on-demand publication services such as Lulu.com (LINK). More recently, electronic book readers such as the Amazon Kindle which store hundreds of books on a single device and which allow readers to directly download books and newspapers have become popular.

(b) Broadcast Media

1. Television : Television has been entertaining American families for over fifty years. In the beginning, there were few programs to pick from, but today, there are hundreds of general and speciality channels to choose from and thousands upon thousands of programs. Where it was once the case that programs had to be watched at the time they were broadcast on television, this is no longer the case. Today, viewers can summon a movie or television episode whenever they want, through many cable or satellite services' pay-per-view or free on-demand services. They may also download or stream episodes from the Internet and watch them on their computers. Viewers may use DVR (digital video recorder) devices, such as a Tivo to record programs at one time and watch them at another time. Viewers with certain cell phones may even watch programs through their cell phones.

2. Movies : Movies (films) are the oldest form of motion picture technology capable of capturing lifelike video-style images. Originally, movies could only be consumed at a neighbourhood movie theatre, but these days' movies are widely available for people to consume in their homes, on their computers, and even in through their telephones. Commercial movies are broadcast on television, and via cable and satellite services which may feature High Definition (HD) video resolution and sound, essentially allowing the movie theatre experience to be replicated in a home theatre environment. Commercial movies are also distributed on DVD and Blu-Ray disks, which can be rented from stores and through-the-mail services such as Netflix, and through downloadable computer files, which can be legally downloaded from movie rental services such as Amazon and iTunes or streamed through Netflix or on-demand cable services. Home movies produced by amateurs with inexpensive video cameras are now also widely available through video sharing websites such as YouTube.com and Vimeo.com.

3. Video Games: Available since the early 1980s, video games have only grown in popularity among youth. Today's games make use of advanced graphics and processors to enable three-dimensional gameplay featuring highly realistic landscapes and physics simulations, and the ability to compete against other players through a network connection. Modern video games are immersive, exciting and increasingly interactive. Players feel like they are in the situation because of the life-like graphics and sounds. Through video games, youth can extend their pretend play, as they become soldiers, aliens, race car drivers, street fighters, and football players. Popular gaming consoles today include Nintendo Wii, Microsoft Xbox 360 and Sony PlayStation III. There are also handheld consoles which enable mobile gameplay such as Nintendo's DS. As well, some video games can also be played on personal computers. Most video games use a hand-held device with buttons, joysticks, and other devices for manipulating the characters on the screen. However, the newer games systems use motion-detecting sensors, such as accelerometers which encourage players to move their entire body to complete game activities. For example, in Wii Tennis, a player swings his entire arm to have the player on the screen hit the tennis ball. Games such as the recently popular World of Warcraft are played in a networked universe shared simultaneously by thousands of gamers at once. Players may be across the street from one another or across the globe using the Internet to participate in a shared three-dimensional world in which each player can control one or more avatars, and chat using text or voice.

(c) Social media

Social media is becoming one of the most popular and most accessed media of communication these days. Social media has brought different people from different geographical area on one platform on which they can share their feeling, ideas, emotions, information and much more. The Manifold social networking sites like Facebook, WhatsApp, Instagram, Twitter, LinkedIn, Google+, and others open the door to share ideas, views, and thoughts on the same platform. With the advancement of science and technology, the world has come close to each other. Today people don't have to wait for the dissemination process but the condition is such that every social media user has become a source of information on their own. The daily news and views to which the social media user comes across to cover a wide range of topics. These topics or subjects are related to the happenings of our surrounding. People can like, show emotions through the list of emoticons or even comment accordingly. The social media act as an umbrella that constitutes a variety of interesting features that have our life very easier. Features of tagging friends, location sharing, photo and video uploads, message chatting, video calling, searching friends etc. have made our life more engaging.

4.26. THE MEDIA AS GATEKEEPER

In addition to the functions discussed previously, media outlets also serve a gatekeeping function, which means they affect or control the information that is transmitted to their audiences. This function has been analyzed and discussed by mass communication scholars for decades. Overall, the mass media serves four gatekeeping functions: relaying, limiting, expanding, and reinterpreting (Bittner, 1996). In terms of relaying, mass media requires some third party to get a message from one human to the next. Whereas interpersonal communication only requires some channel or sensory route, mass media messages need to "hitch a ride" on an additional channel to be received. For example, a Sports Illustrated cover story that you read at SI.com went through several human "gates," including a writer, editor, publisher, photographer, and webmaster, as well as one media "gate" — the Internet. We also require more than sensory ability to receive mass media messages. While hearing and/or sight is typically all that's needed to understand what someone standing in front of you is saying, you'll need a computer, smartphone, or tablet to pick up that SI.com cover story. In summary, relaying refers to the gatekeeping function of transmitting a message, which usually requires technology and equipment that the media outlet controls and has access to, but we do not. Although we relay messages in other forms of communication such as interpersonal and small group, we are primarily receivers when it comes to mass communication, which makes us depend on the gatekeeper to relay the message.

In terms of the gatekeeping function of limiting, media outlets decide whether or not to pass something along to the media channel so it can be relayed. Because most commercial media space is so limited and expensive, almost every message we receive is edited, which is inherently limiting. A limited message doesn't necessarily mean the message is bad or manipulated, as editing is a necessity. But a range of forces including time constraints, advertiser pressure, censorship, or personal bias, among others, can influence editing choices. Limiting based on bias or self-interest isn't necessarily bad as long as those who relay the message don't claim to be objective. Many people choose to engage with media messages that have been limited to match their personal views or preferences. This kind of limiting also allows us to have more control over the media messages we receive. For example, niche websites and cable channels allow us to narrow in on already-limited content, so we don't have to sift through everything on our own.

Gatekeepers also function to expand messages. For example, a blogger may take a story from a more traditional news source and fact check it or do additional research, interview additional sources, and post it on his or her blog. In this case, expanding helps us get more information than we would otherwise so we can be better informed. On the other hand, a gatekeeper who expands a message by falsifying evidence or making up details either to appear more credible or to mislead others is being unethical.

Last, gatekeepers function to reinterpret mass media messages. Reinterpretation is useful when gatekeepers translate a message from something too complex or foreign for us to understand into something meaningful. In the lead-up to the Supreme Court's June 2012 ruling on President Obama's health-care-overhaul bill, the media came under scrutiny for not doing a better job of informing the public about the core content and implications of the legislation that had been passed. Given that policy, language is difficult for many to understand and that legislation contains many details that may not be important to average people, a concise and lay reinterpretation of the content by the gatekeepers (the media outlets) would have helped the public better understand the bill. Of course, when media outlets reinterpret content to the point that it is untruthful or misleading, they are not ethically fulfilling the gatekeeping function of reinterpretation. In each of these gatekeeping functions, the media can fulfil or fail to fulfil its role as the "fourth estate" of government — or government "watchdog." You can read more about this role in the "Getting Critical" box.

4.27. SOCIAL RESPONSIBILITY OF MEDIA

Media's Social Responsibility is one of the four normative theories along with the other three theories, Authoritarian, Libertarian and Marxist theory. The normative theory of media was propounded by Peterson, Wilbur Schramm, and Fred in the1950's. The philosophy of social responsibility depicts the duties of media towards the society; these duties are the collective guidelines of ethics through which Media resolves the conflict and response in tragic times. Social responsibility of media is related to the public opinion and audience reaction on major social interests. Pro-people and society-friendly are important approaches to the media social responsible theory. The theory stated that freedom of media always comes with specific responsibilities towards society.

Prof. Denis Mc Quails (2010) has given some concrete concepts about media social responsibilities in his book 'Mass communication theories.' Mc Quails (2010) wrote that "Media should always show their gratitude towards the society. Media should be unbiased and focus on objectivity with balance approaches". Media should endeavour an appropriate platform to the public where they can express their needs and views on a particular issue. With the concluding note, McQuail (2010) wrote that "media should be liable and accountable to the society." In the past few decades, the opinion of society has changed towards the media. Now, the media is not merely reflective of society.

They also provide a forum for discussion and act as a watchdog of society. In 1947 there was a committee in the USA headed by Robert Hutchins on the freedom of the press. An issue called "who is the journalist responsible to" was in the mainframe of discussion in this committee. Report of Hutchins committee stated that a media person enjoyed the freedom of expression given by the constitution. Undoubtedly, media should be accountable towards society, and they must work as the catalyst for promoting issues of public interest. Normally, media covers the political and socio-economic activities of the society. Media keeps the socio-political facts under their surveillance, but the current media trends are problematic. The media today is only doing 'statement journalism.' Statement journalism is media reporting of any issue without any in-depth analysis. So, instead of behaving as a watchdog of society, media is behaving like a spokesperson. Thus, the main objective of media which serve the society is being replaced by profit-oriented business dealing.

This business and the profit-oriented industrial sector has a concrete relationship with media. As an integral part of society, the industrial sector also has some responsibilities towards society. Media and industrial sector relationship are based on real facts, data, and clarity. Media critics said that a healthy correlation between media and industries might lead to a healthy social impact. Industries are also a major unit of society helpful in fulfilling the financial needs of the society. So while in striving for the betterment of society, media should also provide adequate space for corporate social responsibility in their representation. The media must make the industrial sector accountable for society.

Media also provides a platform for communication between citizens and the corporate sector. The corporate sector should use this platform to create awareness among the citizens regarding their activities and plans. The media platform may also be used by the corporate sector to get feedback from citizens. Hence, the media can work for the development of society as the fourth pillar of society. As an important part of the society, media takes the responsibility to expose the malpractices in the industrial sector and thereby fulfilling their social responsibilities. It is found during the researcher goes the research that the media was instrumental in bringing out the faults of UCIL on their coverage. A critically involved media in society creates a transparent societal system. Unbiased coverage of an industrial disaster and corporate responsibility could help to achieve long-term objectives of a society. A subjective media corporate coverage could lead to many community problems which may eventually result in an industrial disaster like the Bhopal gas tragedy.

4.28. USES OF GRATIFICATION THEORY

Katz and Blumer propounded Uses and Gratification Theory in 1974. Uses and Gratification Theory determines and describes the reach of particular media and audience and vice-versa. It also finds the reasons behind why certain mass has chosen certain media. According to media scholars, the theory has some keys points: Firstly, theory considers the audience as participating elements of mass media; the second step of the theory emphasized the selection of best medium according to their needs. The media cannot satisfy the audience fully. However, the audience is quite aware of their requirements. Gratification from mass media is connected to the audience's necessities. Information, education, and entertainment are common gratification uses of mass through media. Uses and gratification are a two-way process; the first public must actively endeavour their requirements or needs to be gratified through media. For this study, Uses and gratification are one of the most quintessential theories to understand how Bhopal gas victims use the media and gratify them in and after the gas tragedy. The researcher studied the print media impact as uses and gratification of gas survivor after the long period after the lethal accident in Bhopal's union carbide plant in 1984. Although there are lots of debates conducted on the precision and rationale to examine the public use of media; but media experts consistently claim this theory as a valid tool for evaluating the public utilization from various media. Most of the eminent scholars of media consider this theory as an important parameter to judge the social gratification from mass media. Few of them advised that uses and gratification studies are one of the best ways to explore a new horizon in understanding the impact of mass media on society. From the viewpoint of this research, uses and gratification theory examines the public use of media and benefits in the sense of their effects.

Uses and Gratification Theory is based on the selection of media content by an individual according to their requirements. The reason to select a particular medium for any specific needs is dependent on the social situation and psychological status of an individual. The question of how media affects the public and what the public do with the media is the central theme of this thesis. Uses and gratification theory explores both of these aspects and assures great potential of knowledge regarding the effect and reflect the study of media over society. Talking about the uses of the print media Berelson (1952) wrote in his paper 'what missing the newspapers' that "any person read any particular newspaper for some reasons." An individual seeks information and interpretation, especially about public affairs from the newspaper, he further added. Apart from the basic requirements, people also read the newspaper for sensational and mind-boggling stories which appeal to them or connect with them. In the process of communication different mass medium has different target audiences. Print media is most effective in certain circumstances like locality and proximity.

4.29. MEDIA DEPENDENCY THEORY

Sandra Ball- Rokeach and Melvin DE fleur (1976) developed the media dependency theory. As we know that Person, society and media are three major elements of the social system and are interdependent. Co-relationship of individual, media and society is the core element of this theory. Inter-relationship of these components are based on satisfying their communicational needs. Rokeach and DE Fleur (1976), define the dependency theory as "it is a kind of inter-dependency in which gratification of necessity or the accomplishment of the objective of a particular party is dependent over amenity of next party."

As Loges and Rokeach (1993) define the relationship of above-mentioned levels "the assumption of an individual to the media system in helping to achieve his goal could develop the dependency relations with the media. And then as the unit of society individual consider media as most helpful to attain his goal" in their paper Dependency relations and newspaper readership. The researcher found that victims of Bhopal tragedy developed a relationship with the media system for their rehabilitation requirements. Theorists of media dependency also examine the relationship between media, audiences, and society through their background situations. They also explain the future possible correlation situation.

Some studies on the Media Dependency theory found that the public dependency on media is equally proportionate to the degree of the critical situation of society. If the situation of society will be critical or vulnerable, then the degree of dependency of the audience will be more on the media. It reveals that people are not only heavily dependent on media but have expressed their trust in the media. The dependency of people on the media is even more in dreadful situations. The theorist De-Fleur and Rokeach (1976) emphasized the importance of news and their correct implementation which lay the foundation for healthy social relations. The theorist of MDT believes that dependency relationship is a vice-versa of a two-way process. As a basic approach, audiences depend on media for their needs. Media content could be modified by the audience's feedback is the second approach to a two-way process. Thus, it shows the media dependency theory performs various roles to articulate and define the media alliance, and induce social responsibility for the betterment of the media policy concerning the society and individuals.

4.30. AUDIENCE ANALYSIS

One of the consequences of the First Amendment to the Constitution, which protects our right to speak freely, is that we focus so much on what we want to say that we often overlook the question of who our audience is. Does your audience care what you as a speaker think? Can they see how your speech applies to their lives and interests? The act of public speaking is a shared activity that involves interaction between speaker and audience. For your speech to get a fair hearing, you need to create a relationship with your listeners. Scholars Sprague, Stuart, and Bodary explain, "Speakers do not give speeches to audiences; they jointly create meaning with audiences." Sprague, J., Stuart, D., & Bodary, D. (2010). The speaker's handbook (9th ed.). Boston, MA: Wadsworth Cengage. The success of your speech rests in large part on how your audience receives and understands it.

Think of a time when you heard a speech that sounded "canned" or that fell flat because the audience didn't "get it." Chances are that this happened because the speaker neglected to consider that public speaking is an audience-centred activity. Worse, lack of consideration for one's audience can result in the embarrassment of alienating listeners by telling a joke they don't appreciate, or using language they find offensive. The best way to reduce the risk of such situations is to conduct an audience analysis as you prepare your speech.

Audience analysis is the process of gathering information about the people in your audience so that you can understand their needs, expectations, beliefs, values, attitudes, and likely opinions. In this chapter, we will first examine some reasons why audience analysis is important. We will then describe three different types of audience analysis and some techniques to use in conducting audience analysis. Finally, we will explain how you can use your audience analysis not only during the creation of your speech but also while you are delivering it.

4.31. REASONS FOR AN AUDIENCE ANALYSIS

Audience Analysis is conducted for the following reasons.

(a) Acknowledge the Audience : Picture yourself in front of the audience, about to deliver your speech. This is the moment when your relationship with your audience begins, and the quality of this relationship will influence how receptive they will be to your ideas, or at least how willing they'll be to listen to what you have to say. One of the best ways to initiate this relationship is by finding a way to acknowledge your audience. This can be as simple as establishing eye contact and thanking them for coming to hear your presentation. If they've braved bad weather, are missing a world-class sports event, or are putting up with an inconvenience such as a stuffy conference room, tell them how much you appreciate their presence despite the circumstances. This can go a long way toward getting them "on board" with your message.

For a political candidate who is travelling from town to town giving what may be perceived as the same campaign speech time and time again, a statement like "It's great to be here in Springfield, and I want to thank the West Valley League of Women Voters and our hosts, the Downtown Senior Center, for the opportunity to be with you today" lets the audience know that the candidate has at least taken the trouble to tailor the speech to the present audience. Stephanie Coopman and James Lull tell us that Microsoft chairman Bill Gates often adapts to his audiences by thanking them for their participation in the computer industry or for their preparation to participate in an electronic world. The authors say, "Even those brief acknowledgements let audience members know that Gates had prepared his speech with them in mind. "coopman, S. J., & Lull, J. (2009). Public speaking:

(b) Choose a Worthwhile Topic : Your selection of a topic should reflect your regard for the audience. There is no universal list of good or bad topics, but you have an ethical responsibility to select a topic that will be worth listening to. As a student, you are probably sensitive to how unpleasant it would be to listen to a speech on a highly complex or technical topic that you found impossible to understand. However, have you considered that audiences do not want to waste their time or attention listening to a speech that is too simple? Many students find themselves tempted to choose an easy topic or a topic they already know a great deal about. This is an understandable temptation; if you are like most students, you have many commitments and the demands on your time are considerable. Many experts encourage students to begin with something they already know. However, our experience tells us that students often do this simply to reduce their workload. For example, if the purpose of your speech is to inform or persuade students in your public speaking class, a topic such as fitness, drunk driving, the Greek system (campus fraternities and sororities), or credit card responsibility may be easy for you to address, but it is unlikely to go very far toward informing your audience, and in all likelihood, it will not be persuading them either. Instead, your audience members and your professor will quickly recognize that you were thinking of your own needs rather than those of your audience.

To avoid this trap, it behoves you to seek a topic that will be novel and interesting both for you and for your audience. It will also be important to do some credible research to ensure that even the most informed audience members will learn something from you. Many topics could provide a refreshing departure from your usual academic studies. Topics such as the Bermuda Triangle, biopiracy, the environmental niche of sharks, the green lifestyle, and the historic Oneida Community all provide interesting views of human and natural phenomena not usually provided in public education. Such topics might be more likely to hold the interest of your classroom audience than topics they've heard about time and time again.

You should be aware that your audience will not have the same set of knowledge that you do. For instance, if you are speaking about biopiracy, you should probably define it and give a clear example. If your speech is on the green lifestyle, it would be important to frame it as a realistic choice, not a goal so remote as to be hopeless. In each case, you should use audience analysis to consider how your audience will respond to you, your topic, and your message.

(c) **Clarity:** Nothing is more lamentable than a rhetorical actor who endeavours to make grandiose the impressions of others through the utilization of an elephantine albeit nonsensical argot — or nothing is worse than a speaker who tries to impress the audience with a giant vocabulary that no one understands. In the first portion of the preceding sentence, we pulled out as many polysyllabic words as we could find. Unfortunately, most people will just find the sentence wordy and the meaning will pass right over their heads. As such, we as public speakers must ensure that we are clear in what we say. Make sure that you state your topic clearly at the outset, using words that your audience will understand. Letting them know what to expect from your speech shows consideration for them as listeners and lets them know that you value their time and attention.

Throughout your speech, define your terms clearly and carefully to avoid misleading or alarming people by mistake. Be careful not to use jargon or "insider" language that will exclude listeners who aren't "in the know." If you approach audience analysis in haste, you might find yourself presenting a speech with no clear message. You might avoid making any statements outright from fear of offending. It is much better to know to whom you're speaking and to present a clear, decisive message that lets listeners know what you think.

(d) **Controversial Topics Are Important and Risky:** Some of the most interesting topics are controversial. They are controversial topics because people have deeply felt values and beliefs on different sides of those topics. For instance, before you choose nuclear energy as your topic, investigate the many voices speaking out both in favour and against increasing its use. Many people perceive nuclear energy as a clean, reliable, and much-needed source of energy. Others say that even the mining of uranium is harmful to the environment, that we lack satisfactory solutions for storing nuclear waste, and that nuclear power plants are vulnerable to errors and attacks. Another group might view the issue economically, believing that the industry needs nuclear energy. Engineers might believe that if the national grid could be modernized, we would have enough energy and that we should strive to use and waste less energy until modernization is feasible. Some might feel deep concern about our reliance on foreign oil. Others might view nuclear energy as more tried-and-true than other alternatives. The topic is extremely controversial, and yet it is interesting and very important.

(e) Adapt Your Speech to Audience Needs : When preparing a speech for a classroom audience consisting of other students and your professor, you may feel that you know their interests and expectations fairly well. However, we learn public speaking to be able to address other audiences where we can do some good. In some cases, your audience might consist of young children who are not ready to accept the fact that a whale is not a fish or that the moon is always round even though it sometimes appears to be a crescent or a half-circle. In other cases, your audience might include retirees living on fixed incomes and who therefore might not agree that raising local taxes is a vital "investment in the future."

Even in an audience that appears to be homogeneous — composed of people who are very similar to one another — different listeners will understand the same ideas in different ways. Every member of every audience has his or her frame of reference — the unique set of perspectives, experience, knowledge, and values belonging to every individual. An audience member who has been in a car accident caused by a drunk driver might not appreciate a lighthearted joke about barhopping. Similarly, stressing the importance of graduate school might be discouraging to audience members who don't know whether they can even afford to stay in college to complete an undergraduate degree.

These examples illustrate why audience analysis—the process of learning all you reasonably can about your audience—is so centrally important. Audience analysis includes consideration of demographic information, such as the gender, age range, marital status, race, and ethnicity of the people in your audience. Another, perhaps less obvious, demographic factor is socioeconomic status, which refers to a combination of characteristics including income, wealth, level of education, and occupational prestige. Each of these dimensions gives you some information about which kinds of topics, and which aspects of various topics, will be well received.

Suppose you are preparing to give an informative speech about early childhood health care. If your audience is a group of couples who have each recently had a new baby and who live in an affluent suburb, you can expect that they will be young adults with high socioeconomic status; they will likely be eager to know about the very best available health care for their children, whether they are healthy or have various medical problems. In contrast, if your audience is a group of nurses, they may differ in age, but will be similar in education and occupational prestige. They will already know quite a lot about the topic, so you will want to find an aspect that may be new for them, such as community health care resources for families with limited financial resources or for referring children with special needs. As another example, if you are addressing a city council committee that is considering whether to fund a children's health care initiative, your audience is likely to have very mixed demographics.

Audience analysis also takes into account what market researchers call psychographic information, which is more personal and more difficult to predict than demographics.

Psychographic information involves the beliefs, attitudes, and values that your audience members embrace. Respecting your audience means that you avoid offending, excluding, or trivializing the beliefs and values they hold. Returning to the topic of early childhood health care, you can expect new parents to be passionate about wanting the best for their child. The psychographics of a group of nurses would revolve around their professional competence and the need to provide a "standard of care" for their patients. In a city council committee meeting, the topic of early childhood health care may be a highly personal and emotional issue for some of your listeners, while for others it may be strictly a matter of dollars and cents.

(f) Consider Audience Diversity : Diversity is a key dimension of audience members and, therefore, of audience analysis. While the term "diversity" is often used to refer to racial and ethnic minorities, it is important to realize that audiences can be diverse in many other ways as well. Being mindful of diversity means being respectful of all people and striving to avoid racism, ethnocentrism, sexism, ageism, elitism, and other assumptions. An interesting "ism" that is not often mentioned is Chrono centrism or the assumption that people today are superior to people who lived in earlier eras. Russell, J. (1991). Inventing the flat earth. History Today, 41(8), 13-19.

Sociologists John R. Logan and Wenquan Zhang analyzed racial and ethnic diversity in US cities and observed a pattern that rewrites the traditional "rules" of neighbourhood change. Logan, J. R., and Zhang, C. (2010). Global neighbourhoods: New pathways to diversity and separation. American Journal of Sociology, 115, 1069-1109. Whereas in our grandparents' day a racially mixed neighbourhood was one with African American and white residents, in recent decades, many more people from a variety of Asian and Latin American countries have immigrated to the

United States. As a result, many cities have neighbourhoods that are richly diverse with Asian, Hispanic, and African American cultural influences as well as those of white European Americans. Each cultural group consists of people from many communities and occupations. Each cultural group came to the United States for different reasons and came from different communities and occupations within their original cultures. Even though it can be easy to assume that people from a culture are exactly like each other, we undermine our credibility when we create our message as though members of these cultures are carbon copies of each other.

4.32. SPSS.11

SPSS means "Statistical Package for the Social Sciences" and was first launched in 1968. Since SPSS was acquired by IBM in 2009, it's officially known as IBM SPSS Statistics but most users still just refer to it as "SPSS". Six different windows can be opened when using SPSS. The following will describe each of them.

(a) **The Data Editor:** The Data Editor is a spreadsheet in which you define your variables and enter data. Each row corresponds to a case while each column represents a variable. The title bar displays the name of the open data file or "Untitled" if the file has not yet been saved. This window opens automatically when SPSS is started.

(b) **The Output Navigator :** The Output Navigator window displays the statistical results, tables, and charts from the analysis you performed. An Output Navigator window opens automatically when you run a procedure that generates output. In the Output Navigator windows, you can edit, move, delete and copy your results in a Microsoft Explorer-like environment.

(c) **The Pivot Table Editor :** Output displayed in pivot tables can be modified in many ways with the Pivot Table Editor.

You can edit text, swap data in rows and columns, add colour, create multidimensional tables, and selectively hide and show results.

(d) The Chart Editor : We can modify and save high-resolution charts and plots by invoking the Chart Editor for a certain chart (by double-clicking the chart) in an Output Navigator window. You can change the colours, select different type fonts or sizes, switch the horizontal and vertical axes, rotate 3-D scatterplots, and change the chart type.

(e) The Text Output Editor: Text output not displayed in pivot tables can be modified with the Text Output Editor. You can edit the output and change font characteristics (type, style, colour, size).

(f) The Syntax Editor: We can paste your dialogue box selections into a Syntax Editor window, where your selections appear in the form of command syntax.

When creating or accessing data in SPSS, the Data Editor window is used.

Creating a New Data Set

Three steps must be followed to create a new data set in SPSS. The following the tutorial will list the steps needed and will give an example of creating a new data set.

Step 1: Defining Variables in a New Data Set

Variables are defined one at a time using the Define Variable dialogue box. This box assigns data definition information to variables. To access the Define Variable dialogue box, double click on the top of a column where the word var appears or select Define Variable from the Data menu.

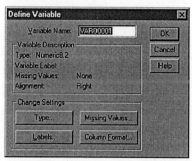

Fig. 4.4. Variable Description

Variable Name : This field describes the name of the variable being defined. To change the name, place the cursor in this field and type the name. The variable name must begin with a letter of the alphabet and cannot exceed 8 characters. Spaces are not allowed within the variable name. Each variable name must be unique.

Type : This field describes the type of variable that is being defined. To change this field, click on the Type... button. This will open the Define Variable Type: dialogue box. Select the appropriate type of data. When done, click on the Continue button.

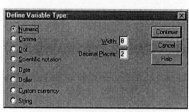

Fig. 4.5. Variable Types

Variable Label: There are two types of variable labels:

1. Variable Label: A name for the variable that can be up to 120 characters long and can include spaces (which variable names cannot). If a variable label is entered, the label will be printed on charts and reports instead of the name, making them easier to understand

Value Label : Provides a key for translating numeric data.

To change the variable label, click on the Labels... button. This will open the Define Labels: dialogue box. Enter the appropriate information into the fields. When done, click on the Continue button.

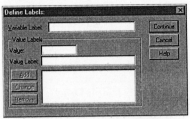

Fig. 4.6. Missing variables

Missing Values: This field indicates which subset of the data will not be included in the data set. To change this field, click on the Missing Values... button. This will open the Define Missing Values: dialogue box. Enter the appropriate information into the fields. When done, click on the Continue button.

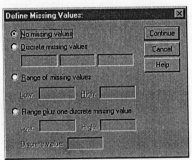

Fig. 4.7. Missing Values

Alignment: This field indicates column alignment and width. To change this field, click on the Column Format... button. This will open the Define Column Format: dialogue box. Enter the appropriate information into the fields. When done, click on the Continue button.

Fig. 4.8. Column Format

(g) Entering Data in a New Data Set : Once all of the variables are defined, enter the data manually (assuming that the data is not already in an external file). The data is typed into the spreadsheet one cell at a time. Each cell represents an observation. When information is typed into a cell, it appears in the edit area at the top of the window. The information is entered into the cell when the active cell is changed. The mouse and the tab, enter, and cursor keys can be used to enter data. To indicate a cell that does not have a data value, a period is entered. A period represents the system-missing value.

(h) Saving a New Data Set : Work performed on a data set only lasts during the current session. To retain the current data set, it must be saved to a file.

1. Select Save from the File menu. The Save Data As dialogue box opens.
2. From the Save as Type drop-down list, select SPSS (*.sav).
3. From the Save in a drop-down list, select the path where the file will be saved.
4. In the File name box, enter a name for the file. SPSS automatically adds the extension. sav.
5. Click Save.

(i) Creating a New Data Set from Other File Formats : SPSS is designed to handle a wide variety of formats including:
- Spreadsheet files created with Lotus 1-2-3 and Excel
- Database files created with dBase
- Tab-delaminated and other types of ASCII text files
- SPSS data files created on other operating systems
- SYSTAT data files

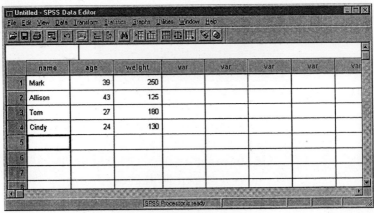

Fig. 4.9. SPSS Data Editor

Opening an Existing SPSS Data Set

1. Select Open from the File menu. This will open the Open File dialogue box.

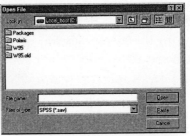

Fig. 4.10. Opening of SPSS File

2. From the Files of type drop-down list, select. sav.
3. From the Look in the drop-down list, select the appropriate drive where the file is located.
4. In the File name box, type in the name of the file to be opened.
5. Click Open.

Printing a Data Set

1. Highlight the data that will be printed. To print all of the data, ignore this step and continue to step 2.

2. Select Print from the File menu. The Print dialogue box opens. Change the options where appropriate.

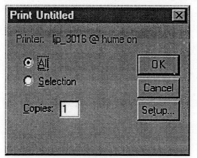

Fig. 4.11

3. Click OK.

   i. Mean, Sum, Standard Deviation, Variance, Minimum Value, Maximum Value, and Range

When generating these statistics, the Data Editor must be open with the appropriate data set before continuing.

Problem: Using the data in the file nba.txt that is located in ~/SPSS/, determine the mean, sum, standard deviation, variance, minimum value, maximum value, and range for height only.

Solution:

1. From the Statistics menu, select Summarize. From the Summarize drop-down menu, select Descriptive. This will open the Descriptive dialogue box.

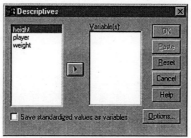

Fig. 4.12. Descriptives

2. In the variable list, select the variable height. Left-click

198   A Textbook of User Studies and Informetrics

on the right arrow button between the boxes to move this variable over to the Variable(s) box. To calculate statistics for many variables, simultaneously add variables to the Variable(s) box.

3. Click on the Options button. This will open the Descriptive: Options dialogue box.

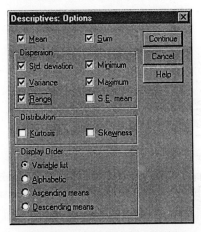

Fig. 4.13. Descriptives option

Click on mean, sum, standard deviation, variance, minimum value, maximum value, and range.

Click on the Continue button when done.

4. Click OK. The descriptive dialogue box closes and SPSS activates the Output Navigator to illustrate the statistics

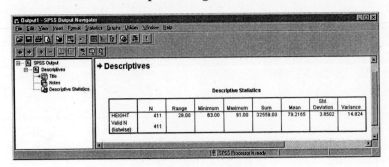

Fig. 4.14. Window Output

A Textbook of User Studies and Informetrics   199

Correlation: Two or more variables may be included in a correlation matrix. When generating the correlation matrix, the Data Editor must be open with the appropriate data set before continuing.

Problem: Using the data in the file nba.txt that is located in ~/SPSS/, determine the correlation between a player's height and weight.

Solution:

1. From the Statistics menu, select Correlate. From the Correlate drop-down menu, select Bivariate. This will open the Bivariate Correlations dialogue box.

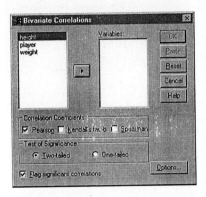

Fig. 4.15. Bivariate Correlations

In the variable list, select height and weight. Left-click on the right arrow button between the boxes to move a variable over to the Variable(s) box.

Select the type of correlation coefficients that will be generated. In this case, use Pearson.

Select the test of significance to be used. In this case, use two-tailed.

Checkmark the Flag significant correlations box.

Click on the Options...button. This will open the Bivariate Correlations: Options dialogue box.

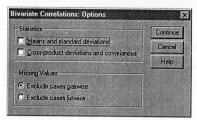

Fig. 4.16. Bivariate Correlations Options

To display the mean and standard deviation for each variable, select Means and standard deviations. In this case, this option is not used.

To display cross-product deviations and covariances for each pair of variables, select Cross-product deviations and covariances. In this case, this option will not be used. When done, click the Continue button.

Click OK. The Bivariate Correlations dialogue box closes and SPSS activates the Output Navigator. The correlation coefficient for each pair of variables is displayed. The number of cases appears at the bottom.

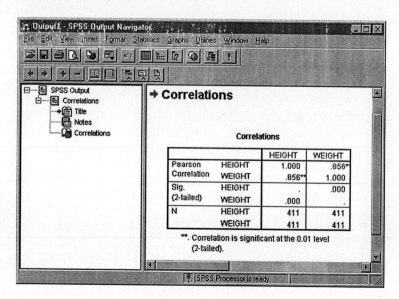

Fig. 4.17. Bivariate Correlations Output

How to Generate Scatter Plots?

Problem: Using the data in ~/SPSS/nba.txt, create an x-y plot of a player's weight versus height.

Solution:

1. From the Graphs menu, select Scatter... This will open the Scatterplot dialogue box.

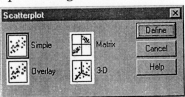

Fig. 4.18. Scatterplot

Select the Simple icon and click Define. This will open the Simple Scatterplot dialogue box.

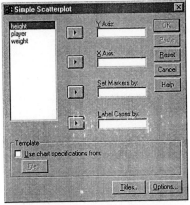

Fig. 4.19. Sample Scatterplot

From the variable list, select weight. Left-click on the right arrow button between the variable list and the Y-Axis box to move the variable, weight, to this box.

From the variable list, select height. Left-click on the right arrow button between the variable list and the X-Axis box to move the variable, height, to this box.

Click on the Options... button. This will open the Options dialogue box.

202   A Textbook of User Studies and Informetrics

Fig. 4.20. Options in the Dialog box

To display a report of missing values, select Display groups defined by missing values. In this case, this option will not be used.

When done, click the Continue button.

To display titles, subtitles, or footnotes on the histogram, click on the Titles... button. This will open the Titles dialogue box.

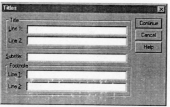

Fig. 4.21. Titles of Analysis

In the Line 1 box, type "Scatter Plot Height vs. Weight".

When done, click the Continue button.

Click OK. The Simple Scatterplot dialogue box closes and SPSS activates the Output Navigator Output window

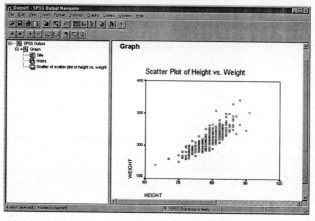

REVIEW QUESTIONS
1. What is the inferential analysis?
2. What is the significance of estimation in decision making?
3. What is interval estimation?
4. State the determining factors in sample size
5. What are the tests of significance?
6. Distinguish between standard deviation and standard error
7. What are type I and type ii errors?
8. Distinguish between standard deviation and standard error
9. What are the assumptions invariance test?
10. What are the steps independent sample test
11. What is f-ratio?
12. What are the dependent samples?
13. How he data edited in SPSS
14. What is the procedure in creating variable?
15. What are the data restrictions in SPSS?

BIBLIOGRAPHY
1. ACAPS, 2011, Direct Observation and Key Informant Interview Techniques. http://www.acaps.org/img/documents/direct-observation-and-key-informant-interview techniques-direct-observation-and-key-informant-interview-techniques.pdf
2. ACAPS Secondary Data Review Technical Brief, June 2011. http://www.acaps.org/img/documents/secondary-data-review – summary-secondary-data-review – summary.pdf
3. Arney, W. R. Understanding Statistics in the Social Sciences. New York: W. H. Freeman, 1990
4. Berthouex, P. M.; L. C. Brown. Statistics for Environmental Engineers. Lewis Publishers, 1994.
5. Box, G. E. P.; W. G. Hunter; J. S. Hunter. Statistics for Experimenters: An Introduction to Design, Data Analysis, and Model Building. John Wiley & Sons, 1978.
6. Bevington, P. R.; D. K. Robinson. Data Reduction and Error Analysis for the Physical Sciences. McGraw-Hill, Inc. 1992
7. Cohen, J., and P. Cohen. Applied Multiple Regression/Correlation Analysis for the Behavioral Sciences. Hillsdale, N.J.: Lawrence Erlbaum Associates, 1975.

8. Devore, J.; N. Farnum. Applied Statistics for Engineers and Scientists. Duxbury Press, 1999.
9. Draper, N., and H. Smith. Applied Regression Analysis, 2nd ed. New York: John Wiley, 1981
10. Family Health International, Qualitative Research Methods: a data collector's field guide, 2005.
11. Freedman, D., R. Pisani, and R. Purves. Statistics. New York: W. W. Norton, 1980
12. Hoaglin, D. C., F. Mosteller, and J. W. Tukey (eds). Exploring Data Tables, Trends, and Shapes. New York: John Wiley, 1985.
13. Line, M. B. (1970). The half-life of periodical literature: Apparent and real obsolescence. Journal of Documentation, 26, 46-52.
14. Kerlinger, F. N. Foundations of Behavioral Research, 3rd ed. New York: Holt, Rinehart and Winston, 1986.
15. Little, R. J. A., and D. B. Rubin. Statistical Analysis with Missing Data. New York: John Wiley, 1987.
16. McBean, E. A.; F. A. Rovers. Statistical Procedures for Analysis of Environmental Monitoring Data & Risk Assessment. Prentice-Hall, 1998.
17. Pillai Sudhier, K. G., & Dileep Kumar, V. (2010). Scientometric study of doctoral dissertations in biochemistry in the University of Kerala, India. Library Philosophy and Practice
18. RANGANATHAN (SR). Library and its scope 7th Annual seminar paper DA1969. Documentation Research and Training Centre, Bangalore; 285-301.
19. Tesch, R. Qualitative Research: Analysis Types and Software Tools. New York: Falmer Press, 1990.
20. Wyverkens E, Provoost V, Ravelingien A, De Sutter P, Pennings G, Buysse A. Beyond sperm cells: a qualitative study on constructed meanings of the sperm donor in lesbian families. Hum Reprod 2014;29:1248–1254.

Unit 5

OBJECTIVES
- To understand the Citation Analysis
- To know the different forms of citations
- Citation counts & Self-citation
- Application of Quantitative and Qualitative techniques in LIS Research
- To explore parametric and non-parametric tools.

5.1. INTRODUCTION

The citation analysis method requires the analysis of the bibliographical references that are usually appended with every research communication. Analysis of such citation can reveal useful information like the relative use of different kinds of documents such as books, periodicals, reports, patents etc., the age of the document which reveals the rate of obsolescence of literature, the most frequently used periodicals, scattering literature, language preference, etc., with different kinds of scientific communities according to subjects, nationality etc., Guha (1983) has rightly said "this type of information can be utilized for the acquisition of materials, selection of periodical, titles, judicious distribution of library funds and so on. Guha (1983) further says " citation studies being indirect, can completely ensure the elimination of bias inherent in most of the direct methods. Such studies are based on records which have already been created. At the same time, citation studies can be much more broad-based than the library record, hence findings of such studies can be said to be valid within a context". Citation analysis reveals only a part cannot give us an insight into the functioning of the entire communication systems and its components e.g. citation counting cannot reveal the use of secondary or tertiary sources nor the use of different channels of communication which are available to any user to go to the primary sources. Such studies are based on individual citation practices of authors where variation is suspected to prevail.

From the application point of view, citation analysis may be considered as a collaborative peer effort to analyze and promote the quality of scholarly publication and research. Citation analysis studies the patterns of citations in documents, an objective method for gathering data about information needs. Meho has observed that citation analysis is a branch of information science in which researchers study the way articles in a scholarly field are accessed and referenced by others. It has been used for scholarly analysis and evaluation in several fields of human endeavour.

5.2. DEFINITION OF CITATION ANALYSIS

Citation analysis is an aspect of bibliometrics, which studies the references used in documents. It uses citations in scholarly works to establish a link to other works or other researchers. Citation analysis is one of the most widely used methods of bibliometrics. Ramesh and Nagaraju defined citation analysis is an activity involving analysis of the citations or references, which form a part of the primary scientific communication. According to Richard citation analysis is the examination of the frequency, patterns, and graphs of citations in articles and books. Smith said that citation analysis is a tool for measuring library collection use. It has been applied to the evaluation of journal collection, for deciding whether to acquire, continue, or discontinue the subscription.

Citation analysis employs bibliographic data from journal articles, monographs, published bibliographies, and electronic indexes to explain trends in-library use. A considerable body of literature exists which uses citation analysis methods as the basis of collection management decisions involving monographs and serials. Research using citations from thesis trends to focus on collection management or evaluation issues and almost exclusively uses citations to examine collection patterns at a particular institution. Citation analysis is known to be a low-cost method whereby a researcher can gather and study citation data in an unobtrusive and non-invasive way. Citation analysis is also a flexible method: it can be applied to the assessment of data sources of a group of libraries, or a single collection or a library collection supplemented with external information sources. It is also flexible in terms of the size of samples, types of citation sources (whether a standard list or a specific collection within a library) as well as the manner of citation selection.

5.3. IMPORTANT AREAS OF CITATION ANALYSIS

(a) Degree of Collaboration Studies

According to Arora and Pawan, increase in multiple authorship and collaboration between researchers is an indication of growing professionalism in different fields. The extent of collaboration in research can be measured with the help of multi authorship of articles. The degree of collaboration among authors is calculated by the following formula given by Subramanyam.

$$C = Nm / (Nm + Ns)$$

Where C = Degree of collaboration in a discipline;

Nm = Number of multi-authored research articles in the discipline published during a year; and

Ns = Number of single-authored research articles in the discipline published during the same year.

Self-Citation Studies: The term „self-citation has been used with different meanings. If the citing paper has one or more authors in common with the cited paper one usually describes this feature as self-citation. However, references to articles published in the same journal in which the citing article appears are also said to be self-citation. When citations are used for science policy purposes, citations of articles authored by people working in the same scientific institution or the same research group as the citing author are also called „self-citations . Self-citations are a special type of citations. Several forms of self-citations can be distinguished; two of them are of special importance: author self-citations and journal self-citations.

Author self-citation occurs if an author referees to their paper, that is if he was the author of one of the co-authors of the cited paper. The spectrum of these self-citations ranged from the obvious case, if an author refers to his work, to more hidden forms, if the co-authors of the author in question are citing him or themselves in another paper. Journal self-citation occurs if a paper published in a given journal is cited by a paper published in the same journal. A great share of journal self-citation allows the conclusion that the journal in question is highly specialized, a low share indicates in a sense a "Lack of originality"; a low share of journal self-citation is characteristic for review journals.

Journal self-citations are also interesting in the context of obsolescence studies. Ageing of journal self-citations can significantly differ from that of „foreign publications. Several bibliometrics is inclined to omit at least the obvious types of author self-citations. In the evaluative context at the micro-level, this practice seems to be justified. Above all, users in science policy, but sometimes even the researchers themselves are almost "condemning" author self-citation as possible means of artificially inflating citation rates and thus of strengthening the authors own position in the scientific community. Other bibliometrics is rather inclined to regard a reasonable share of author self-citations as a natural part of scientific communication. According to this view, it is quite normal that a scientist or a research group refers to their work. Thus, self-citations do not reveal much about the true impact of research. The share of self-citations in all citations as well as their share in all references reveals interesting aspects of an author's or a research groups role in the system of science communication.

(b) Obsolescence / Aging Studies

Obsolescence study of literature is one of the main areas of informetrics and it became an important characteristic of scientific and technological literature. The focus of most of the obsolescence studies is at the individual document level and may extend up to the journal, sub-disciplines or discipline level. The growth of literature and their obsolescence are usually treated together because they represent the initial and final stages of the information cycle. Both are more time-dependent than most other areas of informetrics, where time is not treated as a variable but more as a boundary defining which data are collected.

Obsolescence could be treated as an aspect of citation analysis for journal articles or resources utilization for monograph sources, but the focus is on the tail end of the information life cycle, where document usage on the number of citations received slows down to a point where for all purposes the document is no longer cited. The adjective "obsolete" means the out-of-date, no longer in use, no longer valid or no longer fashionable. The noun "obsolescence" means the process of becoming obsolete; falling into disuse or becoming out of date. Backland explained obsolescence as the relative decreases in the use of the material as it ages. It is the process by which a material becomes no longer useful or reliable63. The term obsolescence is a commonly used notion with a negative connotation and is described as the decline of usefulness over time. It can also be described as temporal selectively in the use of articles It is evident that some materials in libraries become out of date as time progresses. This is known as "obsolescence" of literature. Obsolescence has been defined by Line and Sandison as the "decline overtime is the validity of the information." Obsolescence or ageing is influenced by several factors such as

- The social status of the author (s);
- The reputation of the journal;
- The social form of communication, etc.

Obsolescence/ageing studies are one of the important areas of citation analysis in informetrics. Various studies have been done in this area in science and technology, social science and humanities. Obsolescence study of literature, also called ageing study, involves the decline in the use of documents or citation received by documents overtime. Obsolescence has been the concern of librarians for some time because of the overabundance of materials and lack of housing space. Obsolescence study is useful for researchers, librarians and decision-makers of information centres in identifying the practical shelf-life of documents within disciplines and can be used as a decision support tool in the development of retention of back volumes and space planning. It will also help the pioneers in a scientific discipline how far they will go back to obtain a published paper in their field of interest.

(c) Half-life Studies

In analogy with the radioactive decay in nuclear physics, a concept „half-life has been coined in bibliometric to indicate the obsolescence rate of literature. Because it is not possible to estimate the period that a document would require to get half of the total citations it is going to get, an alternative is proposed as a working definition. Accordingly, it is defined as the period taken for getting half of the total citations already received. On this line, the half-life of the literature in a subject is estimated as the minimum age of half of the active literature in the subject. This is better indicated by the term „median citation age rather than half-life. In tune with the statistical measure of central tendency „median which is defined as that value in a series which divides the whole series into two halves, Median citation age can be defined as the age that divides the total number of active documents as indicated by citations in the current papers arranged in the order of their age, into two halves. In the present study, the median citation age is estimated as a measure of the obsolescence rate of literature in horticulture.

In nuclear physics, the concept of half-life is used to describe the decay of radioactive substances. For physicists, it means the time required for 50% of the atoms in a sample of a radioactive source to disintegrate. These physical half-lives are of equal duration, that is, at any given time, the half-life of the remaining materials is the same as the half-life of the source. Analogous to this physical concept, Burton and Kebler[67] defined the half-life of scientific literature as the time during which one-half of all the currently active (=cited) literature is published. They introduced the term "half-life" to describe the quantitative rate of obsolescence of literature. Line defined half-life as "the time during which one-half of the currently active literature was published."

5.4. APPLICATIONS OF CITATION ANALYSIS

Analysis of bibliographical references in journal articles and research papers can give a picture of the actual use of documents. Thus, it is possible to find out the periodicals and other publications which are frequently consulted the language preference and other such useful information which can help in anticipating the demands of the users. Reference counts, popularly known as the technique of citation analysis have been employed as a bibliometric technique for ascertaining the pattern of literature use. There are following several applications of citation analysis

- To show the pattern of relationship between subjects, languages and countries;
- To shed light on the transmission of knowledge;
- To show how the use of literature changes our time;
- To establish „pecking order of countries, languages, or individual item especially periodicals;
- To serve as a guide to coverage of literature by secondary services and retrospective bibliographies;
- To aid librarians, documentalist and information workers in the selection of representative reading materials for acquis ion, and
- To aid librarians in the identification of items (especially periodicals) for withdrawals.

According to Zunde[70], there are three main application areas in citation analysis:
- Qualitative and quantitative evaluation of scientists, publications and scientific institutions;
- Modelling of the historical development of science and technology;
- Information search and retrieval.

Ramesh and Nagaraju noted citation analysis has five main applications:
- Citation analysis is used to study the citation links between scientific paper; technical notes and reviews; for example, it may be used by the periodicals librarian for the study of the structure of literature and to identify core journals;
- Citation analysis provides relevant measures of utility and relationships of journals whose primary function is to communicate research results;
- Citation analysis helps in the identification of key documents and the creation of core lists of journals;
- It helps in clustering of documents according to common references and citations; and
- It provides a study of the attributes of literature including growth rate, obsolescence, citation practices etc.

5.5. REASONS FOR GIVING CITATIONS

Giving citations is a purely private process and therefore, subjective also. There are many reasons why authors cite the works of others. Weinstock (1971) isolates or has given 15 specific reasons for using citations.
- Paying homage to pioneers.
- Giving credit for related work (homage to peers).
- Identifying methodology, equipment etc.,
- Providing background reading.

- Correcting one's work.
- Correcting the work of others.
- Criticizing the work of others.
- Alerting researchers to forthcoming works.
- Substantiating claims.
- Providing leads to poorly disseminated, poorly indexed or un-cited work.
- Authenticating data and classes of fact-physical constant etc.,
- Identifying original publications describing an eponymous concept or term. E.g. Hodgkin's disease.
- Identifying the original publications in which an idea or constant was discussed
- Disclaiming work or ideas of others and
- Disputing priority claims of others.

5.6. THE HETEROGENEITY OF CITATIONS

The signal, or information, conveyed by a citation, or by a count of citations, varies along still other dimensions besides those of reason and motive. A newspaper citation to a scholar's work is a better indication of the popular appeal of his work than a citation in a scholarly citation to that work is, but the latter is a better indication of the work's scholarly character. A citation made by a distinguished scholar or appearing in a high-quality journal is better evidence of the quality of the cited work than a citation by an undistinguished scholar or in an undistinguished journal. A citation by the same or a lower court, for which the cited case is authoritative, is a weaker signal of respect or regard for the cited case or its author than a citation by a higher or coequal court, which is not required as a matter of stare decisis to follow, distinguish, or otherwise refer to the cited case.

The number of citations to a scholarly work or a judicial

opinion may, moreover, reflect adventitious factors, in particular the size of the population of potential citers and the citation conventions of particular disciplines. These factors make comparisons across fields and, because of growth in the number of journals, over time difficult to make. Even within a single field difference in the specialization can confound citation comparisons; other things being equal, more specialized, applied work is cited less often than more general work (such as a survey article or a theoretical article17) — the potential audience is smaller for the former than for the latter. Similarly, methodological articles, and judicial opinions dealing with procedural issues, tend to be cited more frequently than substantive works because they have a broader domain of applicability.

Differences in the vintages of cited works also make comparison difficult. The older the work, the more time it has had to accumulate citations, but the number of citations is apt to be depressed by shifts in interest away from the topic of the cited work or by the appearance of up-to-date substitutes for it. In economic terms, the stock of knowledge capital created by scholarly or judicial activity, just like a stock of physical capital, both is durable and depreciates. A further problem in interpreting the number of citations to work is that it may be difficult to distinguish empirically between a work that is no longer cited because it has been depreciated and a work that has been so influential that the ideas in it are now referred to without citation to the works in which they first appeared, and often without mention of the author's name (the theory of relativity, or the theory of evolution, or the concept of consumer surplus).

5.7. CITATIONS ANALYSIS AS A MANAGEMENT TOOL

When an enterprise produces goods that are sold in an explicit market, the valuation of its output is straightforward, and generally, it is also feasible to determine the contribution of the enterprise's employees and other suppliers to that output. But not all enterprises are of this kind. Two notable exceptions are research universities and appellate courts. A principal output of both types of enterprise is published work that is not sold. This has been thought in some quarters to preclude analyzing the outputs of these institutions in market terms. An economist would be inclined to question this conclusion.

Academics and judges, economists are prone to believe, are not much different in basic tastes and drives from other people, and universities and courts are subject to budget constraints that require economizing activity. Academic and judicial productivity is much discussed, and comparisons (across academics, academic departments, courts, judges) are attempted. The problem is one of measurement rather than of fundamental incentives and constraints. If that problem can be solved, the market for professors and judges can be assimilated to normal labour markets. Citations analysis can make a significant contribution to the solution, and this is important for operating in these markets as well as for understanding their operation. For example, the federal government has for the last fifteen years been encouraging its research laboratories to focus more on research having commercial applications. Has the policy change? been effective? A study of government patents found that government research is indeed being cited more frequently in private patents. The Patent Office has strict requirements about citing the "prior art," as it is called, and this provides a basis for believing that counting citations in patents provide meaningful, though not wholly reliable, information about the utility of the cited inventions. The application of this methodology to the evaluation of research programs, academic or otherwise, is straightforward.

In my work on judicial administration, I have suggested that weighting the number of decisions of a federal court of appeals by the number of citations to those decisions by other courts of appeals, which is to say courts not bound as a matter of stare decisis to follow the cited court's decisions, yields a meaningful measure of judicial output. This measure can be used to compare the productivity of the different courts. It cannot be the complete measure, if only because it implicitly weights unpublished decisions, which are not citable as precedents, at zero, even though they are an important part of the output of modern appellate courts. An unpublished decision resolves a dispute, which is a useful thing to do even though it doesn't create a citable precedent. Some adjustment should be feasible, however, to yield a total productivity figure. And when productivity is regressed on the different production functions of the different courts, it becomes possible to suggest improvements, An even more audacious use of citations as a judicial management tool is to "grade" appellate judges by the number of other court citations to their opinions. Landes, Lessig, and Solimine, in an ambitious study which I'll call "the Landes study" for the sake of brevity, rank federal appellate judges in just this way. There are comparability problems; the judges are appointed at different times and to courts that have different caseloads, and the number of judges, as well as the number of cases, is changing over time. The authors seek to overcome these problems by regressing other-court citations on variables that include — besides the judge himself — the judge's length of service, his court's caseload, the date on which he was appointed, and other factors that are expected to influence the number of citations that the judge would receive were he of average quality. The coefficient on the judge variable thus indicates how many other-court citations are due to his characteristics rather than to the factors that are not judge-specific which influence citations. Since those factors cannot be controlled for perfectly, the ranking that the Lands study produced is at best a rough guide to the relative quality (or influence, or reputation — it is not altogether clear which is being measured) of the judges in the sample. Still, it may well be an improvement over purely qualitative efforts to evaluate appellate judges.

5.8. LIMITATIONS OF CITATION ANALYSIS

The use of citation analysis to infer the scientific impact of scientific publications has been criticized on several grounds. King reviewed some objections to its use for performance assessment in scientific research:

- Citation analysis assumes that referenced articles disclosed knowledge that was essential to the work depicted in the citing article. Although it is true of most citations, some of them will be "perfunctory."
- Incorrect work may be highly cited. However, it has been argued that cited work, even if incorrect, has made an impact or has stimulated further research efforts whereas poor quality work will usually be ignored.
- Researchers may artificially increase their scientific impact by citing their work. By removing self-citations, the indicator used in any study may be corrected for this.
- Errors in counting the number of citations of an entity (e.g. institution, country etc.) could occur in the WOS (as it could in any other database) due to indexing errors arising from different ways of citing the name of an author and/or institution or to homograph problems (i.e., authors with the same name).
- Another factor affecting citation counts is the difference in citation practices between disciplinary subfields. For instance, it is well known that mathematicians cite less than biomedical researchers. Hence, one should not directly compare publications and citation counts between subfields. The indicator used in any study corrects for this by normalizing citation counts by subfields.
- The WOS coverage of scientific literature has a bias in

favour of countries that publish in English language journals. The scientific productions published in other languages are often underestimated in the context of international comparisons.

A common misconception about indicators based on citation counts is the idea that they inform of the "quality of the underlying work. These indicators provide a partial measure of the impacts published articles have had on the scientific community. Complementary measures of scientific performance such as publications counts, peer ratings, and distinctive awards/prizes have their own set of limitations; the authors refer readers to King 72 for a thorough discussion on these limitations in the context of research evaluation. As such, citation analysis should be used as one of many partial indicators of scientific performance in the toolbox of research evaluators rather than as a stand-alone tool. When all of the indicators converse, the conclusions drawn from the evaluation are regarded as being more reliable than those based on a single indicator.

In the course of doing research, we are called on to summarize our observations, to estimate their reliability, to make comparisons, and to draw inferences. Measures of central tendency such as the mean, median, and mode summarize the performance level of a group of scores, and measures of variability describe the spread of scores among participants. Both are important. One provides information on the level of performance, and the other reveals the consistency of that performance.

5.9. MEASURES OF CENTRAL TENDENCY

(a) The Mean

Two of the most frequently used and most valuable measures of central tendency in psychological research is the mean and median. Both tell us something about the central values or typical measure in a distribution of scores. However, because they are defined differently, these measures often take on different values. The mean, commonly known as the arithmetic average, consists of the sum of all scores divided by the number of scores. Symbolically, this is shown as in which X is the mean; the sign å directs us to sum the values of the variable X.

$$\bar{X} = \frac{\Sigma X}{N}$$

(b) The Median

The median does not use the value of each score in its determination. To find the median, you arrange the values of the variable in order — either ascending or descending — and then count down $(n+1)/2$ scores. This score is the median. If n is an even number, the median is halfway between the two middle scores. Returning to Table 10.1, we find the median gain on a pass play by counting down to the 10.5th case [$(20+1)/2 = 10.5$)]. This is halfway between the 10th and 11th scores. Because both are 0, the median gain is 0. Similarly, the median gain on a running play is The median is a particularly useful measure of central tendency when there are extreme scores at one end of a distribution. Such distributions are said to be skewed in the direction of the extreme scores. The median, unlike the mean, is unaffected by these scores; thus, it is more likely than the mean to be representative of central tendency in a skewed distribution. Variables that have restrictions at one end of distribution but not at the other are prime candidates for the median as a measure of central tendency. A few examples are time scores (0 is the theoretical lower limit and there is no limit at the upper end), income (no one earns less than 0 but some earn in the millions), and the number of children in a family (many have 0 but only one is known to have achieved the record of 69 by the same mother).

(c) The Mode

A rarely used measure of central tendency, the mode simply represents the most frequent score in a distribution. Thus, the model for pass plays is 0, and the mode for running plays is The mode does not consider the values of any scores other than the most frequent score. The mode is most useful when summarizing data measured on a nominal scale of measurement. It can also be valuable to describe a multimodal distribution, one in which the scores tend to occur most frequently around 2 or 3 points in the distribution.

(d) Measures of Variability

We have already seen that a measure of central tendency by itself provides only a limited amount of information about a distribution. To complete the description, it is necessary to have some idea of how the scores are distributed about the central value. If they are widely dispersed, as with the pass plays, we say that variability is high. If they are distributed compactly about the central value, as with the running plays, we refer to the variability as low. But high and low are descriptive words without precise quantitative meaning. Just as we needed a quantitative measure of centrality, so also do we require a quantitative index of variability.

(e) The Range

One simple measure of variability is the range, defined as the difference between the highest and lowest scores in a distribution. Thus, referring to Table 10.1, we see that the range for pass plays is 31 − (−17) = 48; for running plays, it is 10 − 0 = 10. As you can see, the range provides a quick estimate of the variability of the two distributions. However, the range is determined by only the two most extreme scores. At times this may convey misleading impressions of total variability, particularly if one or both of these extreme scores are rare or unusual occurrences. For this and other reasons, the range finds limited use as a measure of variability.

(f) The Variance and Standard Deviation

Two closely related measures of variability overcome these disadvantages of the range: variance and standard deviation. Unlike the range, they both make use of all the scores in their computation. Indeed, both are based on the squared deviations of the scores in the distribution from the mean of the distribution.

Importance of Variability : Why is variability such an important concept? In research, it represents the noisy background out of which we are trying to detect a coherent signal. Look again at Figure 10.1. Is it not clear that the mean is a more coherent representation of the typical results of a running play than is the mean of a pass play? When variability is large, it is simply more difficult to regard a measure of central tendency as a dependable guide to representative performance. This also applies to detecting the effects of an experimental treatment. This task is very much like distinguishing two or more radio signals in the presence of static. In this analogy, the effects of the experimental variable (treatment) represent the radio signals, and the variability is the static If the radio signal is strong, relative to the static, it is easily detected; but if the radio signal is weak, relative to the static, the signal may be lost in a barrage of noise.

In short, two factors are commonly involved in assessing the effects of an experimental variable: a measure of centrality, such as the mean, median, or proportion; and a measure of variability, such as the standard deviation. Broadly speaking, the investigator exercises little control over the measure of centrality. If the effect of the treatment is large, the differences in measures of central tendency will generally be large. In contrast, control over variability is possible. Indeed, much of this text focuses, directly or indirectly, on procedures for reducing variability—for example, selecting a reliable dependent variable, providing uniform instructions and standardized experimental procedures, and controlling obtrusive and extraneous experimental stimuli. We wish to limit the extent of this unsystematic variability for much the same reasons that a radio operator wishes to limit static or noise — to permit better detection of a treatment effect in the one case and a radio signal in the other. The lower the unsystematic variability (random error), the more sensitive is our statistical test to treatment effects.

5.10. INFERENTIAL STATISTICS

From Descriptions to Inferences We have examined several descriptive statistics that we use to make sense out of a mass of raw data. We have briefly reviewed the calculation and interpretation of statistics that are used to describe both the central tendency of a distribution of scores or quantities (mean, median, and mode) and the dispersion of scores around the central tendency (range, standard deviation, and variance). Our goal in descriptive statistics is to describe, with both accuracy and economy of statement, aspects of samples selected from the population. It should be clear that our primary focus is not on the sample statistics themselves. Their value lies primarily in the light that they may shed on characteristics of the population. Thus, we are not interested, as such, in the fact that the mean of the control group was higher or lower than the mean of an experimental group, nor that a sample of 100 voters revealed a higher proportion favouring Candidate A. Rather, our focus shifts from near to far vision; it shifts from the sample to the population. We wish to know if we may justifiably conclude that the experimental variable has had an effect, or we wish to predict that Candidate A is likely to win the election. Our descriptive statistics provide a factual basis for the inductive leap from samples to populations. In the remainder of this chapter, we will take a conceptual tour of statistical decision making. The purpose is not to dwell on computational techniques but rather to explore the rationale underlying inferential statistics.

5.11. THE ROLE OF PROBABILITY THEORY

Recall the distinction between deductive and inductive reasoning. With deductive reasoning, the truth of the conclusion is implicit in the assumptions. Either we draw a valid conclusion from the premises, or we do not. There is no in-between ground. This is not the case with inductive or scientific proof. Conclusions do not follow logically from a set of premises. Rather, they represent extensions of or generalizations based on empirical observations. Hence, in contrast to logical proof, scientific or inductive conclusions are not considered valid or invalid in any ultimate sense. Rather than being either right or wrong, we regard scientific propositions as having a given probability of being valid. If observation after observation confirms a proposition, we assign a high probability (approaching 1.00) to the validity of the proposition. If we have deep and abiding reservations about its validity, we may assign a probability that approaches 0. Note, however, we never establish scientific truth, nor do we disprove its validity, with absolute certainty. Most commonly, probabilities are expressed either as a proportion or as a percentage. As the probability of an event approaches 1.00, or 100%, we say that the event is likely to occur. As it approaches 0.00, or 0%, we deem the event unlikely to occur. One way of expressing probability is in terms of the number of events favouring a given outcome relative to the total number of events possible.

5.12. NULL AND ALTERNATIVE HYPOTHESES

Before beginning an experiment, the researcher sets up two mutually exclusive hypotheses. One is a statistical hypothesis that the experimenter expects to reject. It is referred to as the null hypothesis and is usually represented symbolically as Ho. The null hypothesis states some expectation regarding the value of one or more population parameters. Most commonly, it is a hypothesis of no difference (no effect). Let us look at a few examples: If we were testing the honesty of a coin, the null hypothesis (Ho) would read: The coin is unbiased. Stated more precisely, the probability of a head is equal to the probability of a tail: $Ph = Pt = \frac{1}{2} = 0.5$. If we were evaluating the effect of a drug on reaction time, the null hypothesis might read: The drug does not affect reaction time. The important point to remember about the null hypothesis is that it always states some expectation regarding a population parameter — such as the population mean, median, proportion, standard deviation, or variance. It is never stated in terms of the expectations of a sample. For example, we would never state that the sample means (or median or proportion) of one group is equal to the sample mean of another. It is a fact of sampling behaviour that sample statistics are rarely identical, even if selected from the same population. Thus, ten tosses of a single coin will not always yield five heads and five tails. The discipline of statistics sets down the rules for making an inductive leap from sample statistics to population parameters.

The alternative hypothesis (H1) denies the null hypothesis. If the null hypothesis states that there is no difference in the population means from which two samples were drawn, the alternative hypothesis asserts that there is a difference. The alternative hypothesis usually states the investigator's expectations. Indeed, there really would be little sense embarking upon costly and time-consuming research unless we had some reason for expecting that the experimental variable will affect. Let's look at a few examples of alternative hypotheses: In the study aimed at testing the honesty of a coin, the alternative hypothesis would read: $H1: Ph^1 Pt^1 1/2$; the probability of a head is not equal to the probability of a tail, which is not equal to one-half. In the effect of a drug on reaction time, the alternative hypothesis might read: The administration of a given dosage level of a drug affects reaction time.

5.13. THE SAMPLING DISTRIBUTION AND STATISTICAL DECISION MAKING

Now that we have stated our null and alternative hypotheses, where do we go from here? Recall that these hypotheses are mutually exclusive. They are also exhaustive. By exhaustive we mean that no other possibility exists. These two possible outcomes in our statistical decision exhaust all possible outcomes. If the null hypothesis is true, then the alternative hypothesis must be false. Conversely, if the null hypothesis is false, then the alternative hypothesis must be true. Considering these realities, our strategy would appear to be quite straightforward — simply determine whether the null hypothesis is true or false. Unfortunately, there is one further wrinkle.

The null hypothesis can never be proved to be true. How would you go about proving that a drug has no effect, or that males and females are equally intelligent, or that a coin is honest? If you flipped it 1,000,000 times and obtained exactly 500,000 heads, wouldn't that be proof positive? No. It would merely indicate that, if a bias does exist, it must be exceptionally small. But we cannot rule out the possibility that a small bias does exist. Perhaps the next million, 5 million, or 10 billion tosses will reveal this bias. So we have a dilemma. If we have no way of proving one of two mutually exclusive and exhaustive hypotheses, how can we establish which of these alternatives has a higher probability of being true? Fortunately, there is a way out of this dilemma. If we cannot prove the null hypothesis, we can set up conditions that permit us to reject it. For example, if we had tossed the coin 1,000,000 times and obtained 950,000 heads, would anyone seriously doubt the bias of the coin? We would reject the null hypothesis that the coin is honest. The critical factor in this decision is our judgment that an outcome this rare is unlikely to have been the result of chance factors. It happened for a reason, and that reason is to be found in the characteristics of the coin or in the way it was tossed. In this particular example, we did not engage in any formal statistical exercise to reject

5.14. TYPE I ERRORS, TYPE II ERRORS, AND STATISTICAL POWER

As we saw earlier in the chapter, we can make two types of statistical decisions: reject Ho when the probability of the event of interest achieves an acceptable level (usually $p < 0.05$ or $p < 0.01$), or fail to reject Ho when the probability of the event of interest is greater than 'p' value. Each of these decisions carries an associated risk of error. If we reject Ho (conclude that Ho is false) when in fact Ho is true, we have made the error of falsely rejecting the null hypothesis. This type of error is called a **Type I error**. If we fail to reject Ho (we do not assert the alternative hypothesis) when in fact Ho is false, we have made the error of falsely accepting Ho. This type of error is referred to as a **Type II error**.

5.15. META-ANALYSIS

Whereas measures of effect size provide important information for a particular study, meta-analysis is a statistical technique that indicates the size of an effect across the results of many studies. As different researchers continue to explore a particular research question, published studies begin to accumulate. After some time, it is common for someone to publish a review article to summarize the different studies that have been done and their findings. These review articles often reveal mixed findings; that is, some studies report effects, and some do not.

Meta-analysis provides a statistical method for combining the effects across studies to decide whether a particular independent variable affects a particular dependent variable. Essentially, a measure of effect size is calculated for each study and then weighted according to the sample size and quality of the study. These measures are then averaged across studies to produce an overall effect size. This overall value provides a measure of effect size in standard deviation units. Thus, a meta-analysis that produced an effect size of .33 would indicate that the size of the effect is one-third of the average standard deviation across studies.

5.16. PARAMETRIC VERSUS NONPARAMETRIC ANALYSES

Many data are collected in the behavioural sciences that either does not lend themselves to analysis in terms of the normal probability curve or fail to meet the basic assumptions for its use. For example, researchers explore many populations that consist of two categories — for example, yes/no, male/female, heads/tails, right/wrong. Such populations are referred to as dichotomous, or two-category, populations. Other populations consist of more than two categories — for example, political affiliation or year in college. Other data are best expressed in terms of ranks — that is, on ordinal scales. When comparing the attributes of objects, events, or people, we are often unable to specify precise quantitative differences. However, we are frequently able to state-ordered relationships — for example, Event A ranks the highest concerning the attribute in question, Event B the second-highest, and so on. In addition to equivalence and nonequivalence, then, the mathematical relationships germane to such data are "greater than" (>) and "less than" (<). The relationship $a > b$ may mean that a is taller than b, of higher rank than b, more prestigious than b, prettier than b, and so on. Similarly, the relationship $a < b$ may mean that a is less than b, of lower rank than b, less prestigious than b, and so on. Finally, many data collected by psychologists are truly quantitative. They may be meaningfully added, subtracted, multiplied, and divided. These data are measured on a scale with equal intervals between adjacent values — that is, an interval or ratio scale. For example, in a timed task, a difference of 1 second is the same throughout the time scale. Most commonly, parametric statistics are used with such variables. Parametric tests of significance include the t-test and analysis of variance (ANOVA). Parametric tests always involve two assumptions. One is that the populations for the dependent variable are normally distributed. That is, the distribution of scores conforms to a bell-shaped distribution rather some other shape of the distribution (such as positively or negatively skewed, or multimodal). The risk of a no normal distribution is particularly great with small n's. With large n's, the sampling distributions of most statistics approach the normal curve even when the parent distributions deviate considerably from normality. The second assumption is termed homogeneity of variance. Homogeneity of variance is the assumption that the populations for the dependent variable have equal variances. That is, the degree to which the scores are spread out around the mean is the same in the populations represented by the groups in the study. It is worth noting that parametric tests are robust. As long as the assumptions are not seriously violated, the conclusions derived from parametric tests will be accurate. For data measured on a nominal scale, an ordinal scale, an interval scale with a no normal distribution, or a ratio scale with a no normal distribution, the investigator should use nonparametric statistics for the analysis. For data on a nominal scale, nonparametric analyses include the chi-square test for goodness of fit, the chi-square test for independence, the binomial test, and the median test. For data on an ordinal scale or for data on an interval/ratio scale that do not satisfy the assumption of normality, nonparametric analyses include the Wilcoxon test and the Mann–Whitney test. (It is beyond the scope of this text to review the many nonparametric tests that are available. If you wish to read further, you may consult a statistics textbook.)

5.17. SELECTING THE APPROPRIATE ANALYSIS: USING A DECISION TREE

As you can see, deciding on the appropriate descriptive and inferential statistics for a given study is not easy and involves consideration of several factors. To aid in these decisions, we have included several decision trees. Figure 10.7 illustrates how to choose a descriptive statistic. Figure 10.8 illustrates how to choose a parametric statistic to evaluate group differences. Figure 10.9 illustrates how to choose a nonparametric statistic to evaluate group differences. Finally, Figure 10.10 illustrates how to choose a statistic to measure the relationship between two variables.

(a) Students "t" Test

In 1908 William Sealy Gosset, an Englishman publishing under the pseudonym Student developed the t-test and t distribution. (Gosset worked at the Guinness brewery in Dublin and found that existing statistical techniques using large samples were not useful for the small sample sizes that he encountered in his work.) The t distribution is a family of curves in which the number of degrees of freedom (the number of independent observations in the sample minus one) specifies a particular curve. As the sample size (and thus the degrees of freedom) increases, the t distribution approaches the bell shape of the standard normal distribution. In practice, for tests involving the mean of a sample of size greater than 30, the normal distribution is usually applied.

It is usually first to formulate a null hypothesis, which states that there is no effective difference between the observed sample mean and the hypothesized or stated population mean — i.e., that any measured difference is due only to chance. In an agricultural study, for example, the null hypothesis could be that an application of fertilizer has did not affect crop yield, and an experiment would be performed to test whether it has increased the harvest. In general, a t-test may be either two-sided (also termed two-tailed), stating simply that the means are not equivalent, or one-sided, specifying whether the observed mean is larger or smaller than the hypothesized mean. The test statistic t is then calculated. If the observed t-statistic is more extreme than the critical value determined by the appropriate reference distribution, the null hypothesis is rejected. The appropriate reference distribution for the t-statistic is the t distribution. The critical value depends on the significance level of the test (the probability of erroneously rejecting the null hypothesis).

$$t = \frac{\bar{x} - \mu}{s/\sqrt{n}}$$

(b) Paired t-test

A paired t-test is used when we are interested in the difference between two variables for the same subject. Often the two variables are separated by time. For example, in the Dixon and Massey data set we have cholesterol levels in 1952 and cholesterol levels in 1962 for each subject. We may be interested in the difference in cholesterol levels between these two-time points. However, sometimes the two variables are separated by something other than time. For example, subjects with h ACL tears text annotation indicator may be asked to balance on their leg with the torn ACL and then to balance again on their leg without the torn ACL. Then, for each subject, we can then calculate the difference in balancing time between the two legs

$$t = \frac{\bar{d} - \mu_d}{s_d/\sqrt{n}}$$

(c) Binomial test

A one-sample binomial test allows us to test whether the proportion of successes on a two-level categorical dependent variable significantly differs from a hypothesized value

$$P(X) = \frac{n!}{(n-X)!X!} \cdot (p)^X \cdot (q)^{n-X}$$

Assumptions for the Binomial Test

- Items are dichotomous (i.e. there are two of them) and nominal.
- The sample size is significantly less than the population size.
- The sample is a fair representation of the population.
- Sample items are independent (one item has no bearing on the probability of another)

(d) One-Anova

The one-way analysis of variance (ANOVA) is used to determine whether there are any statistically significant differences between the means of two or more independent (unrelated) groups (although you tend to only see it used when there is a minimum of three, rather than two groups). For example, you could use a one-way ANOVA to understand whether exam performance differed based on test anxiety levels amongst students, dividing students into three independent groups (e.g., low, medium and high-stressed students). Also, it is important to realize that the one-way ANOVA is an omnibus test statistic and cannot tell you which specific groups were statistically significantly different from each other; it only tells you that at least two groups were different. Since you may have three, four, five or more groups in your study design, determining which of these groups differ from each other is important

(e) Factorial ANOVA (Two-way Anova)

ANOVA is short for Analysis of Variance. As discussed in the chapter on the one-way ANOVA the main purpose of a one-way ANOVA is to test if two or more groups differ from each other significantly in one or more characteristics. A factorial ANOVA compares means across two or more independent variables. Again, a one-way ANOVA has one independent variable that splits the sample into two or more groups, whereas the factorial ANOVA has two or more independent variables that split the sample into four or more groups. The simplest case of a factorial ANOVA uses two binary variables as independent variables, thus creating four groups within the sample. For some statisticians, the factorial ANOVA doesn't only compare differences but also assumes a cause-effect relationship; this infers that one or more independent, controlled variables (the factors) cause the significant difference of one or more characteristics. The way this works is that the factors sort the data points into one of the groups, causing the difference in the mean value of the groups.

The factorial design has several important features.

- Factorial designs are the ultimate designs of choice whenever we are interested in examining treatment variations.
- Factorial designs are efficient. Instead of conducting a series of independent studies, we are effectively able to combine these studies into one.
- Factorial designs are the only effective way to examine interaction effects.
- The assumptions remain the same as with other designs - normality, independence and equality of variance.

Source of Variation	d.f.	SS	MS	F_0
Factor A (between groups)	a-1	$SSA = \sum_{i=1}^{a} n_i \left(\bar{y}_{i.} - \bar{y}_{..} \right)^2$	$MSA = \dfrac{SSA}{(a-1)}$	$\dfrac{MSA}{MSE}$
Factor B (between groups)	b-1	$SSB = \sum_{j=1}^{b} n_j \left(\bar{y}_{.j} - \bar{y}_{..} \right)^2$	$MSB = \dfrac{SSB}{(b-1)}$	$\dfrac{MSB}{MSE}$
Error (within groups)	(a-1)(b-1)	$SSE = SST - SSA - SSB$	$MSE = \dfrac{SSE}{(a-1)(b-1)}$	
Total	N-1	$SST = \sum_{i=1}^{a}\sum_{j=1}^{n} \left(y_{ij} - \bar{y}_{..} \right)^2$		

(f) Multivariate Anova (MANOVA)

Multivariate ANOVA (MANOVA) extends the capabilities of analysis of variance (ANOVA) by assessing multiple dependent variables simultaneously. ANOVA statistically tests the differences between three or more group means. For example, if you have three different teaching methods and you want to evaluate the average scores for these groups, you can use ANOVA. However, ANOVA does have a drawback. It can assess only one dependent variable at a time. This limitation can be an enormous problem in certain circumstances because it can prevent you from detecting effects that exist. MANOVA provides a solution for some studies. This statistical procedure tests multiple dependent variables at the same time. By doing so, MANOVA can offer several advantages over ANOVA.

Regular ANOVA tests can assess only one dependent variable at a time in your model. Even when you fit a general linear model with multiple independent variables, the model only considers one dependent variable. The problem is that these models can't identify patterns in multiple dependent variables. This restriction can be very problematic in certain cases where a typical ANOVA won't be able to produce statistically significant results. Let's compare ANOVA to MANOVA. MANOVA can detect patterns between multiple dependent variables. But, what does that mean exactly? It sounds complex, but graphs make it easy to understand. Let's work through an example that compares ANOVA to MANOVA. Suppose we are studying three different teaching methods for a course. This variable is our independent variable. We also have student satisfaction scores and test scores. These variables are our dependent variables. We want to determine whether the mean scores for satisfaction and tests differ between the three teaching methods.

(g) Correlation

Correlation is a statistical technique that can show whether and how strongly pairs of variables are related. For example, height and weight are related; taller people tend to be heavier than shorter people. The relationship isn't perfect.

People of the same height vary in weight, and you can easily think of two people you know where the shorter one is heavier than the taller one. Nonetheless, the average weight of people 5'5" is less than the average weight of people 5'6", and their average weight is less than that of people 5'7", etc. Correlation can tell you just how much of the variation in peoples' weights are related to their heights. Although this correlation is fairly obvious your data may contain unsuspected correlations. You may also suspect there are correlations but don't know which are the strongest.

$$r = \frac{n(\Sigma xy) - (\Sigma x)(\Sigma y)}{\sqrt{\left[n\Sigma x^2 - (\Sigma x)^2\right]\left[n\Sigma y^2 - (\Sigma y)^2\right]}}$$

(h) Canonical correlation

Canonical correlation is a multivariate technique used to examine the relationship between two groups of variables. For each set of variables, it creates latent variables and looks at the relationships among the latent variables. It assumes that all variables in the model are interval and normally distributed. Stata requires that each of the two groups of variables is enclosed in parentheses. There need not be an equal number of variables in the two groups. The output above shows the linear combinations corresponding to the first canonical correlation. At the bottom of the output are the two canonical correlations. Because the output from the concur command is lengthy, we will use the can test command to obtain the eigenvalues, F-tests and associated p-values that we want. Note that you do not have to specify a model with either the concur or the can test commands if they are issued after the canon command.

(i) Simple linear regression

Simple linear regression is a statistical method that allows us to summarize and study relationships between two continuous (quantitative) variables: One variable, denoted x, is regarded as the predictor, explanatory, or independent variable. The other variable denoted y is regarded as the response, outcome, or dependent variable. Because the other terms are used less frequently today, we'll use the "predictor" and "response" terms to refer to the variables encountered in this course. The other terms are mentioned only to make you aware of them should you encounter them. Simple linear regression gets its adjective "simple," because it concerns the study of only one predictor variable.

Assumptions of simple linear regression: Simple linear regression is a parametric test, meaning that it makes certain assumptions about the data. These assumptions are:

Homogeneity of variance (homoscedasticity): the size of the error in our prediction doesn't change significantly across the values of the independent variable.

Independence of observations: the observations in the dataset were collected using statistically valid sampling methods, and there are no hidden relationships among observations.

Normality: The data follows a normal distribution.

Linear regression makes one additional assumption:

The relationship between the independent and dependent variable is linear: the line of best fit through the data points is straight (rather than a curve or some sort of grouping factor).

(j) Multiple regression

Multiple regression generally explains the relationship between multiple independent or predictor variables and one dependent or criterion variable. A dependent variable is modelled as a function of several independent variables with corresponding coefficients, along with the constant term. Multiple regression requires two or more predictor variables, and this is why it is called multiple regression.

The multiple regression equation explained above takes the following form:

$$y = b_1x_1 + b_2x_2 + \ldots + b_nx_n + c.$$

Here, b_i's ($i=1,2\ldots n$) are the regression coefficients, which represent the value at which the criterion variable changes when the predictor variable changes.

As an example, let's say that the test score of a student in an exam will be dependent on various factors like his focus while attending the class, his intake of food before the exam and the amount of sleep he gets before the exam. Using this test one can estimate the appropriate relationship among these factors. Multiple regression in SPSS is done by selecting "analyze" from the menu. Then, from analyze, select "regression," and from regression select "linear."

Assumptions: There should be a proper specification of the model in multiple regression. This means that only relevant variables must be included in the model and the model should be reliable.

Linearity must be assumed; the model should be linear. Normality must be assumed in multiple regression. This means that in multiple regression, variables must have a normal distribution.

Homoscedasticity must be assumed; the variance is constant across all levels of the predicted variable. Certain terminologies help in understanding multiple regression. These terminologies are as follows:

The beta value is used in measuring how effectively the predictor variable influences the criterion variable; it is measured in terms of standard deviation.

R is the measure of association between the observed value and the predicted value of the criterion variable. R Square, or R^2, is the square of the measure of association which indicates the percentage of overlap between the predictor variables and the criterion variable. Adjusted R^2 is an estimate of the R^2 if you used this model with a new data set.

(k) Factorial logistic regression

Multinomial Logistic Regression is the regression analysis to conduct when the dependent variable is nominal with more than two levels. Similar to multiple linear regression, multinomial regression is a predictive analysis. Multinomial regression is used to explain the relationship between one nominal dependent variable and one or more independent variables. Standard linear regression requires the dependent variable to be measured on a continuous (interval or ratio) scale. Binary logistic regression assumes that a dependent variable is a stochastic event. The dependent variable describes the outcome of this stochastic event with a density function (a function of cumulated probabilities ranging from 0 to 1). A cut point (e.g., 0.5) can be used to determine which outcome is predicted by the model based on the values of the predictors.

(l) Ordered logistic regression

Ordered logistic regression is used when the dependent variable is ordered, but not continuous. We do not generally recommend categorizing a continuous variable in this way; we are simply creating a variable to use for this example. The results indicate that the overall model is statistically significant ($p < .0000$) Resnik, D. (2000)6., as are each of the predictor variables ($p < .000$). There are two cut-points for this model because there are three levels of the outcome variable. One of the assumptions underlying ordinal logistic (and ordinal probit) regression is that the relationship between each pair of outcome groups is the same. In other words, ordinal logistic regression assumes that the coefficients that describe the relationship between, say, the lowest versus all higher categories of the response variable are the same as those that describe the relationship between the next lowest category and all higher categories, etc. This is called the proportional odds assumption or the parallel regression assumption. Because the relationship between all pairs of groups is the same, there is only one set of coefficients (only one model). If this was not the case, we would need different models (such as a generalized ordered logit model) to describe the relationship between each pair of outcome groups.

(m) Analysis of covariance (ANCOVA)

Analysis of covariance (ANCOVA) is used in examining the differences in the mean values of the dependent variables that are related to the effect of the controlled independent variables while taking into account the influence of the uncontrolled independent variables. The Analysis of covariance (ANCOVA) is used in the field of business. This document will detail the usability of Analysis of covariance (ANCOVA) in market research. Analysis of covariance (ANCOVA) can be used to determine the variation in the intention of the consumer to buy a particular brand concerning different levels of price and the consumer's attitude towards that brand.

Analysis of covariance (ANCOVA) can be used to determine how a change in the price level of a particular commodity will affect the consumption of that commodity by the consumers. Analysis of covariance (ANCOVA) consists of at least one categorical independent variable and at least one interval natured independent variable. In Analysis of covariance (ANCOVA), the categorical independent variable is termed as a factor, whereas the interval natured independent variable is termed as a covariate. The task of the covariate in Analysis of covariance (ANCOVA) is to remove the extraneous variation from the dependent variable. This is done because the effects of the factors are of major concern in the Analysis of covariance (ANCOVA). Analysis of covariance (ANCOVA) is most useful in those cases where the covariate is linearly related to the dependent variables and is not related to the factors. Similar to Analysis of variance (ANOVA), Analysis of covariance (ANCOVA) also assumes similar assumptions. The following are the assumptions of Analysis of Covariance (ANCOVA):

The variance in the Analysis of covariance (ANCOVA) that is being analyzed must be independent. In the case of more than one independent variable, the variance in Analysis of covariance (ANCOVA) must be homogeneous within each cell that is formed by the categorical independent variables. The data should be drawn from the population using random sampling in the Analysis of covariance (ANCOVA). Analysis of covariance (ANCOVA) assumes that the adjusted treatment means those that are being computed or estimated are based on the fact that the variables obtained due to the interaction of covariate are negligible.

The Analysis of covariance (ANCOVA) is done by using linear regression. This means that the Analysis of covariance (ANCOVA) assumes that the relationship between the independent variable and the dependent variable must be linear. In Analysis of covariance (ANCOVA), the different types of the independent variables are assumed to be drawn from the normal population having a mean of zero.

The Analysis of covariance (ANCOVA) assumes that the regression coefficients in every group of the independent variable must be homogeneous.

Analysis of covariance (ANCOVA) is applied when an independent variable has a powerful correlation with the dependent variable. But, it is important to remember that the independent variables in the Analysis of covariance (ANCOVA) do not interact with other independent variables while predicting the value of the dependent variable. Analysis of covariance (ANCOVA) is generally applied to balance the effect of comparatively more powerful non-interacting variables. It is necessary to balance the effect of interaction in the Analysis of covariance (ANCOVA) to avoid uncertainty among the independent variables. Analysis of covariance (ANCOVA) is applied only in those cases where the balanced independent variable is measured on a continuous scale.

Let us assume a researcher wants to determine the effect of in-store promotion on sales revenue. In this case, Analysis of covariance (ANCOVA) is an appropriate technique because the change in the attitude of the consumer towards the store will automatically affect the sales revenue of the store in Analysis of covariance (ANCOVA). Therefore, in Analysis of covariance (ANCOVA), the dependent variable will be the sales revenue of the store. And the independent variable will be the attitude of the consumer in Analysis of covariance (ANCOVA).

Discriminant analysis

Discriminant analysis is a statistical technique used to classify observations into non-overlapping groups, based on scores on one or more quantitative predictor variables.

For example, a doctor could perform a discriminant analysis to identify patients at high or low risk for stroke. The analysis might classify patients into high- or low-risk groups, based on personal attributes (e.g., cholesterol level, body mass) and/or lifestyle behaviours (e.g., minutes of exercise per week, packs of cigarettes per day).

Note: There are several different ways to conduct a discriminant analysis. The approach described in this lesson is based on linear regression.

Two-Group Discriminant Analysis

A common research problem involves classifying observations into one of two groups, based on two or more quantitative, predictor variables.

When there are only two classification groups, discriminant analysis is just multiple regression, with a few tweaks.

- The dependent variable is a dichotomous, *categorical variable* (i.e., a categorical variable that can take on only two values).
- The dependent variable is expressed as a *dummy variable* (having values of 0 or 1).
- Observations are assigned to groups, based on whether the predicted score is closer to 0 or 1.
- The regression equation is called the discriminant function.
- The efficacy of the discriminant function is measured by the proportion of correct assignments.

The biggest difference between discriminant analysis and standard regression analysis is the use of a categorical variable as a dependent variable. Other than that, the two-group discriminant analysis is just like standard multiple regression analysis. The key steps in the analysis are:

- Estimate regression coefficients.
- Define the regression equation, which is the discriminant function.
- Assess the fit of the regression equation to the data.
- Assess the ability of the regression equation to correctly classify observations.
- Assess the relative importance of predictor variables.

The *sample problem* at the end of this lesson illustrates each of the above steps for two-group discriminant analysis.

Multiple Discriminant Analysis

Regression can also be used with more than two classification groups, but the analysis is more complicated. When there are more than two groups, there are also more than two discriminant functions.

For example, suppose you wanted to classify voters into one of three political groups - Democrat, Republican, or

Independent. Using two-group discriminant analysis, you might:
- Define one discriminant function to classify voters as Democrats or non-Democrats.
- Define a second discriminant function to classify non-Democrats as Republicans or Independents.

The maximum number of discriminant functions will equal the number of predictor variables or the number of group categories minus one - whichever is smaller.

With multiple discriminant analysis, the goal is to define discriminant functions that maximize differences between groups and minimize differences within groups. The calculations to do this making use of canonical correlation, a technique that is beyond the scope of this tutorial.

Test Your Understanding

The SAT is an aptitude test taken by high school juniors and seniors. College administrators use the SAT along with high school grade point average (GPA) to predict academic success in college.

The table below shows the SAT score and high school GPA for ten students accepted to Acme College. And it shows whether each student ultimately graduated from college.

Table 5.1. SAT score and high school GPA

Graduate	SAT	GPA
Yes	1300	2.7
Yes	1260	3.7
Yes	1220	2.9
Yes	1180	2.5
Yes	1060	3.9
No	1140	2.1
No	1100	3.5
No	1020	3.3
No	980	2.3
No	940	3.1

For this exercise, using data from the table, we are going to complete the following tasks:
- Define a discriminant function that classifies incoming students as graduates or non-graduates, based on their SAT score and high school GPA.
- Assess the goodness of fit of the discriminant function.
- Assess how well the discriminant function predicts academic performance (i.e., whether the student graduates).
- Assess the contribution of each independent variable (i.e., SAT and GPA) to the prediction.

To accomplish these tasks, we'll use the regression module in Excel. (We explained how to conduct a regression analysis with Excel in a *previous lesson*.)

Dummy Variable Recoding

Look at the data table above. The dependent variable (Graduate) is a categorical variable that takes the values "Yes" or "No". To use that variable in regression analysis, we need to make it a *quantitative variable*.

We can make Graduate a quantitative variable through *dummy variable* recoding. That is, we can express the categorical variable Graduate as a dummy variable (Y), like so:
- Y = 1 for students that graduate.
- Y = 0 for students that do not graduate.

Now, we replace the categorical variable Graduate with the quantitative variable Y in our data table.

Table 5.2

Y	SAT	GPA
1	1300	2.7
1	1260	3.7
1	1220	2.9
1	1180	2.5
1	1060	3.9
0	1140	2.1
0	1100	3.5
0	1020	3.3
0	980	2.3
0	940	3.1

We input data from the above table into our statistical software to conduct a standard regression analysis. Outputs from the analysis include a regression coefficients table, a coefficient of multiple determination, and an overall F-test. We discuss each output below.

Discriminant Function: The first task in our analysis is to define a linear, least-squares regression equation to predict academic performance, based on SAT and GPA. That equation will be our discriminant function. Since we have two independent variables, the equation takes the following form:

$$w = b_0 + b_1 SAT + b_2 GPA$$

In this equation, w is the *predicted* academic performance (i.e., whether the student graduates or not). The independent variables are SAT and GPA. The regression coefficients are b_0, b_1, and b_2. On the right side of the equation, the only unknowns are the regression coefficients; so to specify the equation, we need to assign values to the coefficients.

To assign values to regression coefficients, we consult the regression coefficients table produced by Excel:

Table 5.3

	Coef	Std Err	t Stat	P-value
Intercept	-3.8392	1.334	-2.878	0.024
SAT	0.003233	0.001	3.145	0.016
GPA	0.23955	0.206	1.165	0.282

Here, we see that the regression intercept (b_0) is -3.8392, the regression coefficient for SAT (b_1) is 0.003233, and the regression coefficient for GPA (b_2) is 0.23955. So the least-squares regression equation is:

$$w = -3.8392 + 0.003233 * SAT + 0.23955 * GPA$$

This is the discriminant function that we can use to classify incoming students as likely graduates or non-graduates.

Goodness of Fit: The fact that our discriminant function satisfies a least-squares criterion does not guarantee that it fits the data well or that it will classify students accurately. To assess goodness of fit, researchers look at the coefficient of multiple determination (R^2) and/or they conduct an overall F test.

Coefficient of Multiple Determination: The coefficient of multiple determination measures the proportion of variation in the dependent variable that can be predicted from the set of independent variables in the regression equation. When the regression equation fits the data well, R^2 will be large (i.e., close to 1); and vice versa.

The coefficient of multiple determination is a standard output of Excel (and most other analysis packages), as shown below.

Table 5.4

SUMMARY OUTPUT	
Regression Statistics	
Multiple R	0.781125
R Square	0.610156
Adjusted R Square	0.498772
Standard Error	0.373135
Observations	10

A glance at the output suggests that the regression equation fits the data pretty well. The coefficient of multiple determination is 0.610. This means 61% of the variation in academic performance (i.e., graduating vs. not graduating) can be explained by SAT score and by high school GPA.

Overall F Test : Another way to evaluate the discriminant function would be to assess the statistical significance of the regression sum of squares. For that, we examine the ANOVA table produced by Excel:

Table 5.5

ANOVA	df	SS	MS	F	Sig of F
Regression	2	1.525	0.763	5.478	0.037
Residual	7	0.975	0.139		
Total	9	2.500			

This table tests the statistical significance of the independent variables as predictors of the dependent variable. The last column of the table shows the results of an overall F test. The *p-value* (0.037) is small. This indicates that SAT and/or GPA has explanatory power beyond what would be expected by chance.

Like the coefficient of multiple correlations, the overall F test found in the ANOVA table suggests that the regression equation fits the data well.

The validity of the Discriminant Function : In the real

world, we are probably most interested in how well we can classify observations, based on outputs from the discriminant function. The table below shows actual student performance (Y) and predicted performance (w), computed using the discriminant function.

Table 5.6

Y	w	SAT	GPA
1	0.97	1300	2.7
1	1.08	1260	3.7
1	0.75	1220	2.9
1	0.53	1180	2.5
1	0.48	1060	3.9
0	0.30	1140	2.1
0	0.51	1100	3.5
0	-0.16	1020	3.3
0	0.20	980	2.3
0	-0.10	940	3.1

Recall that the discriminant function was designed to predict 0's and 1's. Thus, if predicted performance (w) is less than 0.5, we assign the student to the "not graduating" group; and if it is greater than 0.5, we assign the student to the "graduating" group.

Comparing actual performance (Y) and predicted performance (w) in the table above, we see that the discriminant function correctly classified eight of ten students. The incorrect classifications are highlighted in grey. One student who did not graduate was incorrectly assigned to the "graduating" group, and one student who graduated was incorrectly assigned to the "not graduating" group.

This result seems to indicate that SAT and GPA are useful in predicting graduation status.

Note: For this hypothetical example, we used the same data (1) to define the discriminant function and (2) to test the discriminant function. This is poor practice because it capitalizes on chance variation in the data set. In the real world, we should use one data set to define the discriminant function and a different data set to test its validity.

Significance of Regression Coefficients : When the discriminant function has more than one independent variable, it is natural to ask whether each independent variable contributes significantly to the regression *after-effects of other variables are taken into account*. The answer to this question can be found in the regression coefficients table:

Table 5.7

	Coef	Std Err	t Stat	P-value
Intercept	-3.839	1.334	-2.878	0.024
SAT	0.0032	0.001	3.145	0.016
GPA	0.2395	0.206	1.165	0.282

The regression coefficients table shows the following information for each coefficient: its value, its standard error, a t-statistic, and the significance of the t-statistic. In this example, the t-statistic for SAT score was statistically significant at the 0.05 level; the t-statistic for GPA was not. This means that the SAT contributed significantly to the regression after-effects of GPA are taken into account.

(b) Factor analysis

Factor analysis is a technique that is used to reduce a large number of variables into fewer numbers of factors. This technique extracts maximum common variance from all variables and puts them into a common score. As an index of all variables, we can use this score for further analysis. Factor analysis is part of the general linear model (GLM) and this method also assumes several assumptions: there is a linear relationship, there is no multicollinearity, it includes relevant variables into the analysis, and there is a true correlation between variables and factors. Several methods are available, but the principal component analysis is used most commonly.

Types of factoring: There are different types of methods used to extract the factor from the data set:

1. Principal component analysis : This is the most common method used by researchers. PCA starts extracting the maximum variance and puts them into the first factor. After that, it removes that variance explained by the first factors and then starts extracting maximum variance for the second factor. This process goes to the last factor.

2. Common factor analysis : The second most preferred method by researchers, it extracts the common variance and puts them into factors. This method does not include the unique variance of all variables. This method is used in SEM.

3. Image factoring : This method is based on the correlation matrix. OLS Regression method is used to predict the factor in image factoring.

4. Maximum likelihood method : This method also works on correlation metric but it uses maximum likelihood method to factor.

5. Other methods of factor analysis : Alfa factoring outweighs least squares. Weight square is another regression-based method which is used for factoring.

Factor loading : Factor loading is the correlation coefficient for the variable and factor. Factor loading shows the variance explained by the variable on that particular factor. In the SEM approach, as a rule of thumb, 0.7 or higher factor loading represents that the factor extracts sufficient variance from that variable.

Eigenvalues : Eigenvalues is also called characteristic roots. Eigenvalues show variance explained by that particular factor out of the total variance. From the commonality column, we can know how much variance is explained by the first factor out of the total variance. For example, if our first factor explains

68% variance out of the total, this means that 32% variance will be explained by the other factor.

Factor score : The factor score is also called the component score. This score is of all row and columns, which can be used as an index of all variables and can be used for further analysis. We can standardize this score by multiplying a common term. With this factor score, whatever analysis we will do, we will assume that all variables will behave as factor scores and will move.

Criteria for determining the number of factors: According to the Kaiser Criterion, Eigenvalues is a good criterion for determining a factor. If Eigenvalues is greater than one, we should consider that a factor and if Eigenvalues is less than one, then we should not consider that a factor. According to the variance extraction rule, it should be more than 0.7. If the variance is less than 0.7, then we should not consider that a factor.

Rotation method : Rotation method makes it more reliable to understand the output. Eigenvalues do not affect the rotation method, but the rotation method affects the Eigenvalues or percentage of variance extracted. There are some rotation methods available: (1) No rotation method, (2) Varimax rotation method, (3) Quartimax rotation method, (4) Direct oblimin rotation method, and (5) Promax rotation method. Each of these can be easily selected in SPSS, and we can compare our variance explained by those particular methods.

Assumptions:
- *No outlier* : Assume that there are no outliers in data.
- *Adequate sample size* : The case must be greater than the factor.
- *No perfect multicollinearity* : Factor analysis is an interdependency technique. There should not be perfect multicollinearity between the variables.
- *Homoscedasticity* : Since factor analysis is a linear function

of measured variables, it does not require homoscedasticity between the variables.
- *Linearity* : Factor analysis is also based on the linearity assumption. Non-linear variables can also be used. After transfer, however, it changes into a linear variable.
- *Interval Data* : Interval data are assumed.

Key concepts and terms

Exploratory factor analysis: Assumes that any indicator or variable may be associated with any factor. This is the most common factor analysis used by researchers and it is not based on any prior theory.

Confirmatory factor analysis (CFA): Used to determine the factor and factor loading of measured variables, and to confirm what is expected on the basic or pre-established theory. CFA assumes that each factor is associated with a specified subset of measured variables. It commonly uses two approaches:

The traditional method : Traditional factor method is based on principal factor analysis method rather than common factor analysis. The traditional method allows the researcher to know more about insight factor loading.

The SEM approach : CFA is an alternative approach of factor analysis which can be done in SEM. In SEM, we will remove all straight arrows from the latent variable, and add only that arrow which has to observe the variable representing the covariance between every pair of latent. We will also leave the straight arrows error-free and disturbance terms to their respective variables. If standardized error term in SEM is less than the absolute value two, then it is assumed good for that factor, and if it is more than two, it means that there is still some unexplained variance which can be explained by factor. Chi-square and some other goodness-of-fit indexes are used to test how well the model fits.

5.17. NON-PARAMETRIC TEST

(a) The Chi-Square Test

The Chi-Square Test of Independence determines whether there is an association between categorical variables (i.e., whether the variables are independent or related). It is a nonparametric test. This test is also known as the Chi-square Test of Association. This test utilizes a contingency table to analyze the data. A contingency table (also known as a *cross-tabulation*, *crosstab*, or *two-way table*) is an arrangement in which data is classified according to two categorical variables. The categories for one variable appear in the rows, and the categories for the other variable appear in columns. Each variable must have two or more categories. Each cell reflects the total count of cases for a specific pair of categories.

The Chi-Square Test of Independence is commonly used to test the following:

Statistical independence or association between two or more categorical variables. The Chi-Square Test of Independence can only compare categorical variables. It cannot make comparisons between continuous variables or between categorical and continuous variables. Additionally, the Chi-Square Test of Independence only assesses associations between categorical variables, and can not provide any inferences about causation. If your categorical variables represent "pre-test" and "post-test" observations, then the chi-square test of independence is not appropriate. This is because the assumption of the independence of observations is violated. In this situation, McNamara's Test is appropriate.

Data must meet the following requirements:
- Two categorical variables.
- Two or more categories (groups) for each variable.
- Independence of observations.

- There is no relationship between the subjects in each group.
- The categorical variables are not "paired" in any way (e.g. pre-test/post-test observations).
- Relatively large sample size.
- Expected frequencies for each cell are at least 1.
- Expected frequencies should be at least 5 for the majority (80%) of the cells.

(b) Wilcoxon-Mann-Whitney test

The modules on hypothesis testing presented techniques for testing the equality of means in two independent samples. An underlying assumption for appropriate use of the tests described was that the continuous outcome was approximately normally distributed or that the samples were sufficiently large (usually $n_1 > 30$ and $n_2 > 30$) to justify their use based on the Central Limit Theorem. When comparing two independent samples when the outcome is not normally distributed and the samples are small, a nonparametric test is appropriate.

A popular nonparametric test to compare outcomes between two independent groups is the Mann Whitney U test. The Mann Whitney U test, sometimes called the Mann Whitney Wilcoxon Test or the Wilcoxon Rank Sum Test, is used to test whether two samples are likely to derive from the same population (i.e., that the two populations have the same shape). Some investigators interpret this test as comparing the medians between the two populations. Recall that the parametric test compares the means (H0: $μ_1=μ_2$) between independent groups. In contrast, the null and two-sided research hypotheses for the nonparametric test are stated as follows:

H0: The two populations are equal versus

H1: The two populations are not equal.

This test is often performed as a two-sided test and, thus, the research hypothesis indicates that the populations are not equal as opposed to specifying directionality. A one-sided research hypothesis is used if interest lies in detecting a positive or negative shift in one population as compared to the other. The procedure for the test involves pooling the observations from the two samples into one combined sample, keeping track of which sample each observation comes from, and then ranking lowest to highest from 1 to n1+n2, respectively

(c) The Kruskal-Wallis H test

The Kruskal-Wallis H test (sometimes also called the "one-way ANOVA on ranks") is a rank-based nonparametric test that can be used to determine if there are statistically significant differences between two or more groups of an independent variable on a continuous or ordinal dependent variable. It is considered the nonparametric alternative to the one-way ANOVA, and an extension of the Mann-Whitney U test to allow the comparison of more than two independent groups. For example, you could use a Kruskal-Wallis H test to understand whether exam performance, measured on a continuous scale from 0-100, differed based on test anxiety levels (i.e., your dependent variable would be "exam performance" and your independent variable would be "test anxiety level", which has three independent groups: students with "low", "medium" and "high" test anxiety levels). Alternately, you could use the Kruskal-Wallis H test to understand whether attitudes towards pay discrimination, where attitudes are measured on an ordinal scale, differed based on job position (i.e., your dependent variable would be "attitudes towards pay discrimination", measured on a 5-point scale from "strongly agree" to "strongly disagree", and your independent variable would be "job description", which has three independent groups: "shop floor", "middle management" and "boardroom").

It is important to realize that the Kruskal-Wallis H test is an omnibus test statistic and cannot tell you which specific groups of your independent variable are statistically significantly different from each other; it only tells you that at least two groups were different. Since you may have three, four, five or more groups in your study design, determining which of these groups differ from each other is important. You can do this using a post hoc test

(d) Jonckheere-Terpstra test

The Jonckheere-Terpstra test is a rank-based nonparametric test that can be used to determine if there is a statistically significant trend between an ordinal independent variable and a continuous or ordinal dependent variable. The Jonckheere-Terpstra test tests for an ordered difference in medians where you need to state the direction of this order (this will become clearer below). It is also known as the Jonckheere-Terpstra test for ordered alternatives.

Note : The Jonckheere-Terpstra test is similar to the Kruskal-Wallis H test, which can be used to determine if there are statistically significant differences between two or more groups of an independent variable on a continuous or ordinal dependent variable. However, unlike the Jonckheere-Terpstra test, the Kruskal-Wallis H test does not predict how the differences in the scores of the dependent variable will depend on the ordinal nature of the groups of the independent variable. This is explained further in the Assumptions section later.

For example, you could use a Jonckheere-Terpstra test to understand whether test scores, measured on a continuous scale from 0-100, differed based on time spent revising (i.e., your dependent variable would be "test score" and your independent variable would be "revision time", which has four ordinal independent groups: "0-5 hours", "6-10 hours", "11-15 hours" and "16-20 hours"). You expect that the median test score increases with increasing hours spent revising.

Alternately, you could use the Jonckheere-Terpstra test to understand whether job satisfaction, measured on an ordinal scale, differed based on job position (i.e., your dependent variable would be "job satisfaction", measured on a 5-point scale from "very satisfied" to "very dissatisfied", and your independent variable would be "job position", which has three ordered independent groups: "Account Executive", "Account Manager" and "Account Director"). You expect job satisfaction to increase with a higher job position.

(e) The Friedman test

The Friedman test is the non-parametric alternative to the one-way ANOVA with repeated measures. It is used to test for differences between groups when the dependent variable being measured is ordinal. It can also be used for continuous data that has violated the assumptions necessary to run the one-way ANOVA with repeated measures (e.g., data that has marked deviations from normality).

Assumptions : When you choose to analyse your data using a Friedman test, part of the process involves checking to make sure that the data you want to analyse can be analysed using a Friedman test. You need to do this because it is only appropriate to use a Friedman test if your data "passes" the following four assumptions:

Assumption #1: One group that is measured on three or more different occasions.

Assumption #2: Group is a random sample from the population.

Assumption #3: Your dependent variable should be measured at the ordinal or continuous level. Examples of ordinal variables include Likert scales (e.g., a 7-point scale from strongly agree through to strongly disagree), amongst other ways of ranking categories (e.g., a 5-point scale explaining how much a customer liked a product, ranging from "Not very much" to "Yes, a lot"). Examples of continuous variables include revision time (measured in hours), intelligence (measured using IQ score), exam performance (measured from 0 to 100), weight (measured in kg), and so forth. You can learn more about ordinal and continuous variables in our article: Types of Variable.

Assumption #4: Samples do NOT need to be normally distributed.

The Friedman test procedure in SPSS Statistics will not test any of the assumptions that are required for this test. In most cases, this is because the assumptions are a methodological or study design issue, and not what SPSS Statistics is designed for. In the case of assessing the types of the variable you are using, SPSS Statistics will not provide you with any errors if you incorrectly label your variables as nominal.

(f) One sample median test

The sign test is a good general non-parametric test, which makes very few assumptions (requirements) but has limited power. To use the sign test you need only know that every pair of data points (observations) are ordered, for instance, x > y. If all your data points (all your observations) can be given a rank value >a value like first, 2nd, 3rd, etc..., and if you have asymmetric distribution, the Wilcoxon signed-rank test can be used. So, since it begins with more assumptions, the Wilcoxon signed-rank test is more specific, with a narrower focus; but it also (usually) has more power to find differences than the more general sign test.

(g) The Fisher Exact test

The Fisher Exact test is a test of significance that is used in the place of the chi-square test in 2 by 2 tables, especially in cases of small samples. Statistics Solutions is the country's leader in fisher exact test and dissertation consulting. Contact Statistics Solutions today for a free 30-minute consultation. The Fisher Exact test tests the probability of getting a table that is as strong due to the chance of sampling. The word 'strong' is defined as the proportion of the cases that are diagonal with most cases. The Fisher Exact test is generally used in one-tailed tests. However, it can also be used as a two-tailed test as well. It is sometimes called a Fisher Irwin test. It is given this name because it was developed at the same time by Fisher, Irwin and Yates in 1930. In SPSS, the Fisher Exact test is computed in addition to the chi-square test for a 2X2 table when the table consists of a cell where the expected number of frequencies is fewer than 5. Certain terminologies help in understanding the theory of the Fisher Exact test.

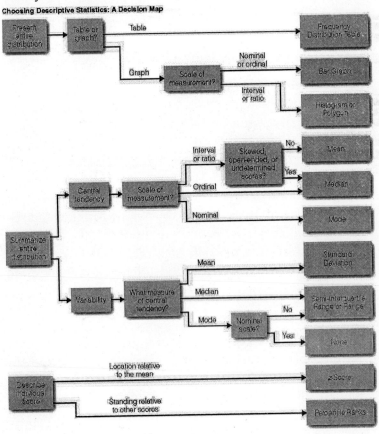

Fig. 5.1

A Textbook of User Studies and Informetrics

Choosing a Parametric Test: A Decision Map for Making Inferences About Population Means or Mean Differences

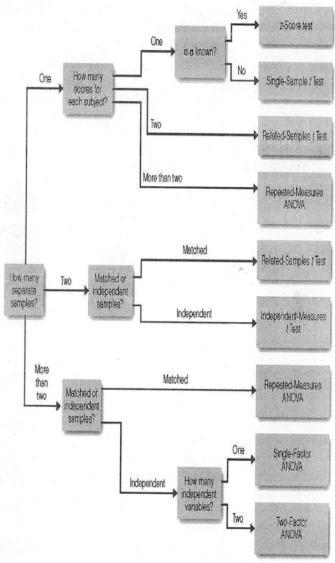

Fig. 5.2

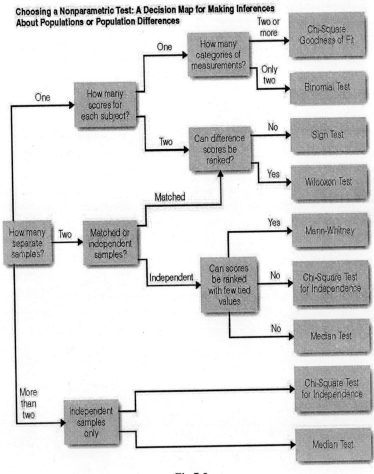

Fig 5.3

5.18. DETAILED SUMMARY

1. Statistics provide an objective approach to understanding and interpreting the behaviours that we observe and measure.

2. Descriptive statistics are used to describe and summarize data. They include measures of central tendency (mean, median, mode) and measures of variability (range, variance, standard deviation).

Descriptive statistics are often presented in the form of graphs.

3. Measures of central tendency indicate the "centre" of the distribution of scores, whereas measures of variability indicate the spread of scores.

4. The mean is the arithmetic average of a set of scores. It considers the precise value of each score in the distribution. It is the preferred measure of central tendency for interval or ratio data unless the distribution of scores is skewed by outlier (extreme) scores.

5. The median is the middle point in the distribution. That is, half of the scores are above the median, and half are below the median.

6. The mode is the most frequent score in the distribution — that is, the score that occurs most often.

7. The range is the number of units between the highest and lowest scores in the distribution. Because the range only considers the values of the two most extreme scores, it is less stable than other measures of variability and may not adequately reflect the overall spread of scores.

8. The variance is the average squared deviation of scores from the mean. The square root of the variance is the standard deviation. Thus, standard deviation reflects, on average, how far scores are from the mean. It is the preferred measure of variability.

9. Many variables result in a distribution of scores that is normal in shape. This observation, along with the calculated mean and standard deviation, provides a wealth of additional information regarding the proportion of scores in particular parts of the distribution or the probability (or percentage chance) of obtaining a particular score in the distribution.

10. Variability is an essential concept in behavioural research because most of the principles of good research

design involve methods to reduce variability due to extraneous variables so that variability due to systematic sources (our independent variables) is clear.

11. Researchers should make extensive use of tables and graphs to summarize data. Such techniques provide the researcher with a better "feel" for the data.

12. We usually research samples of participants and then want to conclude populations. Inferential statistics are tools used to make such inferences.

13. The conclusions made using inferential statistics are based on probabilities — specifically, the probabilities that certain events would occur simply by chance. Thus, our research hypotheses are never proven correct or incorrect. They are either retained or rejected based on probabilities.

14. The null hypothesis typically states that there is no difference in population parameters (usually population means), whereas the alternative hypothesis typically states that there is a difference in population parameters. The null hypothesis is the one that is statistically tested and either retained or rejected, whereas the alternative hypothesis usually reflects the researcher's expectation.

15. The frame of reference for statistical decision making is provided by the sampling distribution of a statistic. A sampling distribution is a theoretical probability distribution of the possible values of some sample statistic that would occur if we were to draw all possible samples of a fixed size from a given population.

16. If the probability of obtaining a sample statistic by chance is very rare, very unlikely, less than our alpha level (often 0.05), then we conclude that the sample did not come from the population and that our independent variable had a significant effect (that is, we reject the null hypothesis).

17. Power is the probability of finding a certain size effect assuming that it exists. Power can be increased by increasing sample size and by using control techniques to reduce extraneous variability.

18. Because all conclusions are based on probabilities, our conclusions can be wrong. If we conclude that there is an effect and there really is not, then we have made a Type I error. If we conclude that there is no effect and there is one, then we have made a Type II error. Good research designs and experimental control will reduce the chance of making these errors.

19. The decision to reject a null hypothesis does not reflect the size of an effect. Other statistics measure effect size, providing another valuable tool in data analysis.

20. A particular inferential technique called meta-analysis provides a statistical method for combining the effects across studies to decide whether a particular independent variable affects a particular dependent variable.

21. Parametric statistics are used when data are measured on an interval or ratio scale and meet a few additional assumptions regarding sample size and variability. Nonparametric statistics are used when data are measured on a nominal or ordinal scale or do not meet the assumptions of parametric statistics.

22. During data analysis, the researcher must decide on the most appropriate descriptive and inferential statistics. These decisions are not always easy, and flowcharts can be a useful aid.

23. Statistical software makes data analysis much more efficient and less prone to errors in calculation. However, it is the responsibility of the researcher to understand what the software is doing to the data and to not blindly click the mouse on a series of buttons.

REVIEW QUESTIONS

1. Explain the importance of citation analysis
2. Narrate the application of citation analysis
3. State reasons for applying the citation analysis
4. What re the limitations of citation analysis?
5. Define the null and alternative hypothesis.
6. What do you understand about type I and type II error?
7. Elucidate the various parametric test normally used by the researchers.
8. State the conditions for applying the non-parametric test.
9. Illuminate the impact of factor analysis
10. Describe the circumstances in which the regression analysis may be used.

BIBLIOGRAPHY

1. Barley, S. R. (1986). Technology as an Occasion for Structuring - Evidence from Observations of CT Scanners and the Social-Order of Radiology Departments. Administrative Science Quarterly, 31(1), 78-108.
2. Bidwell, M. (2009). Do Peripheral Workers Do Peripheral Work? Comparing the Use of Highly Skilled Contractors and Regular Employees. Industrial & Labor Relations Review, 62(2), 200 225
3. Bergsman, H. (2010). External Learning Activities and Team Performance: A Multimethod Field Study. Organization Science, 21(1), 81-96.
4. Briscoe, F. (2007). From iron cage to iron shield? How bureaucracy enables temporal flexibility for professional service workers. Organization Science, 18(2), 297-314.
5. Bryman, A. (2006). Integrating quantitative and qualitative research: How is it done? *Qualitative Research*, 6(1), 97-113.
6. Cameron, W. B. (1963). Informal sociology, a casual introduction to sociological thinking. New York, Random House.
7. Canales, R. (2014). Weaving Straw into Gold: Managing Organizational Tensions Between Standardization and Flexibility in Microfinance. Organization Science, 25(1), 1-28.
8. Creswell, J. W., & Clark, V. L. P. (2007). Designing and conducting mixed methods research. Thousand Oaks, Calif.: SAGE Publications.
9. Denis, J. L., Langley, A., & Rouleau, G. A. (2006). The power of numbers in strategizing. Strategic Organization, 4(4), 349-377.

10. DiMaggio, P., Nag, M., & Bile, D. (2013). Exploiting affinities between topic modelling and the sociological perspective on culture: Application to newspaper coverage of US government arts funding. Poetics, 41(6), 570-606.
11. Doering, L. (2014). Rethinking Escalation of Commitment: Relational Lending in Microfinance. Working Paper.
12. Edmondson, A. (1999, Jun). Psychological safety and learning behaviour in work teams. Administrative Science Quarterly, pp. 350-383
13. Edmondson, A. C., & Mcmanus, S. E. (2007). Methodological fit in management field research. Academy of Management Review, 32(4), 1155-1179.
14. Eisenhardt, K. M., & Bourgeois, L. J., III. (1988). Politics of Strategic Decision Making in High-Velocity Environments: Toward a Midrange Theory. *Academy of Management Journal, 31*(4), 737-770.
15. Elsbach, K. D. (1994). Managing Organizational Legitimacy in the California Cattle Industry – the Construction and Effectiveness of Verbal Accounts. *Administrative Science Quarterly, 39*(1), 57-
16. Ely, R. J. (1994). The Effects of Organizational Demographics and Social Identity on Relationships among Professional Women. *Administrative Science Quarterly, 39*(2), 203-238.
17. Fernandez-Mateo, I. (2009). Cumulative Gender Disadvantage in Contract Employment. *American Journal of Sociology, 114*(4), 871-923.
18. Fine, G. A., & Elsbach, K. D. (2000). Ethnography and experiment in social psychological theory building: Tactics for integrating qualitative field data with quantitative lab data. Journal of Experimental Social Psychology, 36(1), 51-76.
19. Greene, J. C., Caracelli, V. J., & Graham, W. (1989). Toward a conceptual framework for mixed-method evaluation designs. Educational Evaluation and Policy Analysis, 11(3), 255-274.
20. Jick, T. D. (1979). Mixing Qualitative and Quantitative Methods: Triangulation in Action. Administrative Science Quarterly, 24(4), 602-611.
21. Kaplan, S. (2008a). Cognition, capabilities, and incentives: Assessing firm response to the fibre-optic revolution. Academy of Management Journal, 51(4), 672-695.
22. Kaplan, S. (2008b). Framing contests: strategy making under uncertainty. Organization Science, 19(5), 729-752.
23. Kaplan, S., & Vakili, K. (Forthcoming). The double-edged sword of recombination in breakthrough innovation. Strategic Management Journal.

24. Kellogg, K. C. (2009). Operating Room: Relational Spaces and Micro-Institutional Change in Two Surgical Teaching Hospitals. American Journal of Sociology, 115(3), 657-711.
25. Lounsbury, M. (1997). Exploring the institutional tool kit - The rise of recycling in the US solid waste field. American Behavioral Scientist, 40(4), 465-477.
26. Mische, A. (2008). Partisan publics: communication and contention across Brazilian youth activist networks. Princeton: Princeton University Press.
27. Porter, T. M. (1995) Trust in Numbers: The Pursuit of Objectivity in Science and Public Life. Princeton, NJ: Princeton University Press.
28. Ranganathan, A. (2014). Choosing Meaning over Money? Evidence from a Field Audit Study with Handicraft Artisans in Southern India. Working Paper.
29. Sieber, S. D. (1973). Integration of Fieldwork and Survey Methods. American Journal of Sociology,78(6), 1335-1359.
30. Small, M. L. (2011). How to Conduct a Mixed Methods Study: Recent Trends in a Rapidly Growing Literature. Annual Review of Sociology, Vol 37, 37, 57-86...
31. Tripsas, M. (1997). Unravelling the process of creative destruction: Complementary assets and incumbent survival in the typesetter industry. Strategic Management Journal, 18, 119-142.